21 Days To Divine Healing

21 Days To Divine Healing

A BIBLICAL DEVOTIONAL FOR OVERCOMING PAIN, SICKNESS AND DISEASE

Deon O. Thomas

This book is dedicated to my two beautiful, faithful and godly sisters,
Dr. Sherie – Ann Thomas and Dr. Marcelle Thomas. May the Lord use you
both, not only to bring medical help to thousands of patients, but also God's
divine healing to the lives of all those you encounter.

Table of Contents

Foreword

21 DAYS TO DIVINE HEALING is a succinct must-read, especially at this time when the SARS virus, COVID-19, like a new modern plague has taken center stage on the world's platform.

Many people fear this viral disease especially as it has resulted in several deaths. This viral illness targets airway receptors, damages pneumocytes (air cells) in the lungs and causes alveoli to collapse, hence generating oxygen starvation and death. Medical doctors like myself are still learning about this novel, corona virus.

What causes sickness however? The causes of sickness are always multiple. They include the visible that we can see with the naked eye and those (like the viral) for which we need powerful electron microscopes. The causes range from those we know to those for which we still grope in the dark to determine the cause. Not infrequently, even when we do know the cause, the 'WHY factor' still haunts us.

Sickness may also be induced by spiritual factors. Sin, including disunity and divisions in the Christian church caused Paul to tell the Corinthians: "For this cause, many are weak and sickly among you and many sleep" (1 Corinthians 11:30). In this context, the term 'sleep' does not indicate that many were enjoying a temporary nap or a restful snooze. It means that many died! Prior to the Apostle Paul, the prophets of old had warned Israel that, for their sins, God would bring 'wonderful' plagues on them (Deuteronomy 28:59; Jeremiah 24:10).

Here is a book that re-lives the experiences of people who had a range of different diseases. Some would have spent all their financial, social, physical and mental resources to seek help. Some were reduced to being beggars and others were at the point of death! In common, they all had experienced a change of focus but even for those at the point of death, help came.

A change of focus often causes us to turn our eyes outward for help, and many people look to governments for this help. Across the globe, governments spend billions of dollars annually to pay expert advisers and medical personnel; purchase medicines and equipment (e.g. respirators); and procure vaccines for help with such illnesses as the COVID-19 virus. Governments, however, have their limitations. To date, sixty-four million people have been infected with the COVID-19 virus. More than one million have died and the COVID-meter cases continue to surge. Recently, it was reported that in the USA alone in the period of just four days, more than ten thousand people have died from the disease.

21 Days To Divine Healing, like an eye-opener, invites us to peer through a new set of lenses to focus on Jesus, the Great Physician, who heals every disease. People like you and me who had become sick with various diseases, some of whom were even at the point of death, received healing from Him. The truth is that He is able to do exceedingly abundantly above all that we can ask or think! He has not changed.

Read this book and learn how the One who created the heavens and the earth, stands ready to heal physically, mentally and spiritually, all those who truly come to Him in faith, believing in His ability to heal.

Dr. Roy H. Thomas
(M.D., M.A., FRCSEd.)

Acknowledgments

I⸱ᴛ ᴡᴏᴜʟᴅ ʙᴇ ʀᴇᴍɪss ᴏꜰ me not to give a word of thanks to the people who have greatly helped to make this book possible. Special thanks must be given to Mrs. Sadie Thomas, an expert editor, a brilliant mind and one who is dearly loved – my dear mother. She patiently read and edited each page of this manuscript and offered many valuable suggestions. Also, I have to thank my beloved father – Dr. Roy Thomas for taking time out of his busy medical schedule to write the foreword. I must also express my gratitude to Mr. Ronel McLennon who expertly designed the cover for this book. Finally, I have to thank my dear wife, Joanna, for her great patience and understanding which enabled me to have the hours I needed to complete this work in a timely manner.

Introduction

THIS DEVOTIONAL HAS BEEN DIVIDED into 21 brief chapters and each has been specifically designed to accomplish just one task that will help you to experience the healing power of the Lord. Although you could probably read through this devotional in a single sitting, I would definitely hasten to advise you not to do so. Instead of racing to finish it, enjoy the journey. Read only one chapter a day and allow the Word of God to speak to you, challenge you and heal you as you meditate on each day of the journey.

There are a couple of features that have been put into each day to help you receive the maximum benefit from this life-changing devotional:

1. Each chapter begins with a verse or a couple of verses. Do not gloss over them; read them slowly and prayerfully and allow the Lord to speak to you and heal you through them.
2. For each day, there is a thought which relates directly to the verse or verses given. Take your time and make sure you understand what is being said. Re-read the thought for the day and underline those areas that stand out to you.
3. At the end of each thought is a short statement for you to remember. This helps to summarize the thought for the day into one sentence or phrase.
4. For each day, there is a specific challenge designed to help you to walk in God's divine healing. Do the challenges, do NOT skip

    them. They are specifically designed to help you experience God's healing power in your life.

5.   Finally, each chapter has a closing prayer that is designed to do two things: First, it helps those who do not know how to pray to learn to pray and secondly, it acts as a template from which you can start off praying and proceed into your own prayer.

My hope and prayer for you is that as you work through this devotional and put into practice the challenges for each day, you will experience the mighty healing power of the Lord in your life and discover the beauty of God's compassion towards you.

Let us begin our journey!

First Things First

Our Greatest Priority

"I want to know Christ and the power of his resurrection
and the fellowship of sharing in his sufferings,
becoming like him in his death, and so somehow,
to attain to the resurrection from the dead."

PHILIPPIANS 3:10-11

"Because he loves me," says the Lord, "I will rescue him;
I will protect him, for he acknowledges my name."

PSALM 91:14

UNBELIEF IS PERHAPS ONE OF the most common struggles we all have faced at one stage or another in our relationship with the Lord. I am not speaking here of an open denial to the truth of the Word of God, but of an inherent uncertainty that often causes us to ask such questions as:

- Will the Lord answer my prayer to be healed?
- Is He going to heal my child?
- Are my parents going to live through this sickness and be able to play with their grandchildren?
- Will He come through for me on this occasion?
- Why is the Lord taking so long to answer my prayers?

Questions like those flood our hearts, and the solid answers we desire can often escape us. If we are absolutely honest, sometimes our expectations sink so low that we are tempted to embrace whatever we are going through as 'our lot in life'. We might not openly renounce our faith, but in the midst of our discouragement, we may silently struggle to believe the Lord for a favorable outcome.

One of the many reasons such uncertainty abounds is that we have failed to continually grow in our knowledge of who the Lord is. Knowing the Lord should be, and always remain, our first priority. Take a look at what the Word of God says:

"But seek first his kingdom and his righteousness, and all these things will be given to you as well."

Matthew 6:33

As God's creation, knowing the Lord is beyond question our most important responsibility. It is more important than being healed, delivered, financially rewarded, or any of those other wonderful things. Nothing is wrong with any of those things in and of themselves, but when our hearts secretly long for them above the Lord Himself, we fall into the sin of idolatry. Like all other sins, idolatry seeks to deceive us and deprive us of the richest blessings of God in our lives. Look at what the Word of God says:

"Your wrongdoings have kept these away; your sins have deprived you of good."

Jeremiah 5:25

Our only antidote against idolatry is worship – worship of the One and Only true God. When our desire to please Him, and know Him more and more, supersedes our desire to receive from Him, we enter into the world of worship. This is the realm in which we ought to live – in worshipful adoration of the Lord. Like the apostle Paul, the desperate cry of our hearts should be:

"I want to know Christ and the power of his resurrection and the fellowship of sharing in his sufferings, becoming like him in his death, and so somehow, to attain to the resurrection from the dead."

Philippians 3:10-11

Paul understood that the true purpose of life, the only worthwhile endeavor, was to know Jesus Christ. Knowing the Lord was far more important to him than being healed, doing miracles, preaching, or some other ministry related activity. From the depths of his soul, the apostle Paul cried out for an everlasting friendship with Jesus, being fully aware that nothing else could satisfy him.

When we prioritize knowing Jesus, our perspective shifts, our faith increases and those insecurities that once exalted themselves in our hearts and minds disappear. We begin to see Jesus for who He really is, and we come to know that He never changes. The Word of God declares:

"Jesus Christ is the same yesterday and today and forever."

Hebrews 13:8

In light of this truth, we can be certain of what He is going to do because of what He has done.

As you go through this devotional, my prayer is that faith will enter your heart in an increasing measure, and that you will long to know Jesus and experience His healing power in your life. However, you must first address this question:

"Is knowing the Lord my greatest priority?"

Let me make it perfectly clear that many have been healed by the Lord, but have missed the more important blessing of knowing Him. The Lord

4

never manipulates us by withholding healing until we have accepted Jesus as our Lord and Savior, and matured in our love walk with Him. This is certainly not how He operates. The Bible tells us:

"He causes his sun to rise on the evil and the good, and sends rain on the righteous and the unrighteous"

Matthew 5:45b

As you seek the Lord for your healing, however, the full picture must first be embraced. God's foremost mission in our lives is to bring us into the saving knowledge of His Son, Jesus Christ. If you have not yet entered into a relationship with God through faith in Jesus Christ, or if you are a Christian in a backslidden state, I want to urge you to commit your life to the Lord. It always amazes me how willingly the Lord blesses us when we prioritize what is most important to Him.

On this first day of our journey, let us commit ourselves to the Lord. He most certainly wants us to experience His healing power in every area of our lives, but the healing of our eternal souls is of far greater significance in His eyes.

Remember:
As God's creation, knowing the Lord is beyond question our most important responsibility.

Challenge:
Memorize Philippians 3:10-11

"I want to know Christ and the power of his resurrection and the fellowship of sharing in his sufferings, becoming like him in his death, and so somehow, to attain to the resurrection from the dead."

Philippians 3:10-11

PRAYER FOR TODAY

Heavenly Father, I thank You for Your great interest in every area of my life. I thank You for calling me into a real, living relationship with You through faith in Jesus Christ. Father, today I turn away from the sin of idolatry. Too often I desire Your provisions in my life above Your presence, and today, Lord, I commit my whole life to You. Forgive me, Lord, of all my sins. I renounce every way that is not in conformity to Your will. I surrender my life to the Lordship of Jesus Christ and accept You as my Lord and Savior.

Dear Lord, I want to know You and to understand Your ways. As I seek Your face and ask You to heal my body of all sickness, pain and discomfort, I want my heart to be softened towards You, and I want You to **fill** me with a deep and passionate love for You. I also ask You, Lord, to flood my heart with an insatiable desire for Your Word. Thank You, Lord, for who You are, and for Your great interest and love for me. All these things I pray in Jesus' name.

Amen.

The Lord is Good To Me

"Praise the Lord, O my soul; all my inmost being, praise his
holy name. Praise the Lord, O my soul, and forget not all his
benefits – who forgives all your sins and heals all your diseases."

PSALM 103:1-3

"But he was pierced for our transgressions, he was crushed
for our iniquities; the punishment that brought us peace
was upon him, and by his wounds we are healed."

ISAIAH 53:5

IRRESPECTIVE OF ALL THE NEGATIVE experiences we may have had in our
lifetime, or may be going through right now, we have so much for which
to be grateful. If this seems too difficult for you to believe, or you have
been blinded from seeing the innumerable blessings that surround
you, take some time to look at your fingers and thank the good Lord
for each one of them. After that, look at each of the toes on your feet
and thank Him again. Thank Him for your eyes, and for the ability to
see. Thank Him for your mind and for giving you the ability to think
and read the words on the pages of this book. Consider each body part
He has mercifully blessed you with and thank Him. As you consider

all that He has done in simply forming you, you will find that there is so much to be thankful for – indeed we all have good reason to praise the Lord.

The Psalmist, King David, was one who knew very well that God was good and worthy of all praise. In his enthusiasm he boldly declared to himself:

"Praise the Lord, O my soul; all my inmost being, praise his holy name."

Psalm 103:1

David did not have a trouble-free life by any means. He was envied by some of his own brothers, repeatedly threatened by Saul, the first king of Israel, and he also had to face the painful consequences for some of his own failures. Despite all of this, however, he held on to his deep, meaningful relationship with the Lord, and often encouraged himself to give thanks to the Lord regardless of his circumstances. I think you read that last statement too quickly, and so I will write it again. David encouraged HIMSELF to give thanks to the Lord! Even in one of his most stressful situations, the Bible records that David encouraged and strengthened himself in the Lord (1 Samuel 30:6).

Sometimes we will not have anyone encouraging us on our journey towards healing, and we can experience discouragement and be tempted to give up in our pursuit of the promises of the Lord. However, it is in those difficult times that we need to encourage ourselves to declare God's Word and praise Him for who He is. Like the Psalmist David, we need to recall the many benefits that we have as a direct result of our relationship with the Lord.

In Psalm 103, David mentioned at least five benefits he had received from the Lord. Let us take a look at each one of them.

Benefit #1 – The Forgiveness of the Lord
The first benefit David mentioned about the Lord was that He forgives all our sins (Psalm 103:3). This is a tremendous benefit for all of us

who are in right relationship with the Lord. To be forgiven means to be released, set free and cleansed from every stain of sin on our soul. When we confess and renounce our sins, we receive the Lord's forgiveness (Proverbs 28:13), and we will never be judged for those sins.

What a joy it is to be forgiven by the Lord. Those sins covered by the blood of Jesus, which we have confessed and forsaken, will never have the power to stain us and bring us under the judgment of God. Hallelujah!

Benefit #2 – The Lord heals all our diseases
The second benefit that David mentions is that the Lord heals ALL our diseases (Psalm 103:3). This is another great benefit that the Lord bestows on us. There is no sickness that poses a problem for the Lord. He is more than able to heal all our diseases, and we should always expect Him to heal all the pains, sicknesses and ailments in our bodies. Healing is just one of the many benefits of being in right relationship with the Lord.

Benefit #3 – The Lord redeems our life from the pit
When our life is hidden in Christ, we will never end in the pit – a place of utter destruction. It makes absolutely no sense to experience the healing power of God in our earthly life, and spend our eternity in the pit. The Lord who forgives and heals also protects all who have placed their faith in Jesus Christ from eternal damnation. Indeed, the Lord redeems (delivers) us from utter destruction!

Benefit #4 – The Lord showers us with love and compassion
It is an immense benefit to be dearly loved by the Lord. Can you imagine if John 3:16 said: 'For God so hated the world'? We would all be dammed to a hopeless and tormented eternity. Thankfully John 3:16 declares:

> "For God so loved the world that he gave his one and only Son, that whoever believes in him shall not perish but have eternal life"

God loves the world and it was this divine love that was the driving force for sending Jesus, His Son, into the world to die on a cruel cross for the sins of humanity. Not only does the Lord love us but He is also compassionate toward us, which means, He exercises mercy toward us. One of my favorite verses in the Bible declares:

> "He does not treat us as our sins deserve or repay us according to our iniquities"
>
> Psalm 103:10

Indeed the Lord our God is great in His love and compassion toward us!

Benefit #5 – The Lord satisfies our desires with good things

The fifth benefit from the Lord is that He satisfies our desires with good things. Very often, professing Christians doubt that the Lord will do good in their lives. In order to get rid of this deep insecurity we have to learn to immerse our minds in the Word of God and not allow the devil to blind us to the truth of who the Lord is. The Lord is good and He gives good gifts to His people. Look at what the Word of God declares:

> "Every good and perfect gift is from above, coming down from the Father of the heavenly lights, who does not change like shifting shadows."
>
> James 1:17

> "Which of you, if his son asks for bread, will give him a stone? Or is he asks for a fish, will give him a snake? If you, then, though you are evil, know how to give good gifts to your children, how much more will your Father in heaven give good gifts to those who ask him!"
>
> Matthew 7:9-11

God is good and all that He does is good. This is certainly not my opinion but God's Word. Look for yourself:

"You are good, and what you do is good; teach me your decrees."

Psalm 119:68

The Lord our God is good and we can therefore always expect good from Him. As we pray for God's healing power to be manifest in our lives, let us always remember that our Heavenly Father is good, and He will only do what is good for us.

Remember:
The Lord our God is great in His love and compassion toward us.

Challenge:
Memorize Psalm 103:1-3

"Praise the Lord, O my soul; all my inmost being, praise his holy name. Praise the Lord, O my soul, and forget not all his benefits – who forgives all your sins and heals all your diseases."

Psalm 103:1-3

PRAYER FOR TODAY

Heavenly Father, I thank You for Your Word. You are good and all that You do is good. Thank You, Lord, for teaching me from Your Word that I should only expect You to do good to me. In the same manner that a parent would give their child what is good, help me to realize that You are a lot more amazing than any earthly parent, and I can therefore expect Your goodness to be extended to me. Dear Lord, I ask You to completely heal and strengthen my body. All these things I pray in the name of Jesus.

Amen.

Exposure leads to Experience

"Jesus went throughout Galilee, teaching in their
synagogues, preaching the good news of the kingdom,
and healing every disease and sickness among the people.
News about him spread all over Syria, and people brought
to him all who were ill with various diseases, those
suffering severe pain, the demon- possessed, those having
seizures, and the paralyzed, and he healed them."

MATTHEW 4:23-24

"WHEN EVENING CAME, MANY WHO were demon-possessed were brought to
him, and he drove out the spirits with a word and healed all the sick.
This was to fulfill what was spoken through the prophet Isaiah:

"He took up our infirmities and carried our diseases."

Matthew 8:16-17

One verse that has had a profound impact on my life over the years is
Matthew 4:4:

"Man does not live on bread alone, but on every word that comes from the mouth of God."

As true as this statement is, from my experience, I have found that many professing Christians do not actually believe this. Typically, I come across believers who do not faithfully spend time reading the Bible, or ensuring that their every decision in life is grounded upon God's Word. It is therefore not surprising to see numerous local church assemblies filled with individuals who have experienced significant spiritual defeat in their lives. Ignorance of God's Word will always result in very painful, or even fatal consequences. Look at what the Word of God says:

"Take to heart all the words I have solemnly declared to you this day, so that you may command your children to obey carefully all the words of this law. They are not just idle words for you – they are your life. By them you will live long in the land you are crossing the Jordan to possess"

Deuteronomy 32:46-47

In the passage above, Moses was declaring God's loving admonition to the children of Israel as they were about to embark on their journey to the Promised Land. He pleaded with them to take every single word of God seriously because their very life was dependent on it.

There is a strong relationship between our experience of God's Word and our exposure to it. Never forget that! Throughout the synoptic gospels, we see Jesus teaching and preaching the Word of God before we see people experiencing the miraculous power of God's word in their lives. Jesus, the living Word of God (John 1:1), deeply understood the powerful dynamic between the declared Word of God and its impact on the hearers.

The Word of God is unlike any other. When we hear it, it has an effect on us. In fact, the Bible teaches us that, as we hear the Word of God, faith comes into our hearts (Romans 10:17). The intensity of our belief of what the Lord will do in our lives is directly related to the amount of God's Word entering our hearts. It could almost be categorically stated that the primary reason many people struggle to believe in the healing power of God is that they have too little exposure to the Word of God. As we read and meditate on God's Word, we are not merely receiving a history lesson on the mighty works the Lord did in the past. Instead, we discover who the Lord is, learn about His ways and we receive faith to believe that what He did yesterday, He will do today.

In order to experience the healing effect of God's Word in our lives, we first need to be repeatedly exposed to the Scriptures. Jesus could have healed without saying a word, but He chose to operate from the authority of the Word of God. After He declared the Word of God, people would experience the power of God in their lives. They would be healed of various sicknesses, delivered, set free from pain, and also from impure spirits. All these mighty miracles occurred after the Lord preached the life- changing Word of God.

May we continually expose ourselves to the Word of God and experience His mighty miraculous power in our lives.

Remember:
There is a strong relationship between our experience of God's Word and our exposure to it.

Challenge:
Memorize Matthew 4:23-24

"Jesus went throughout Galilee, teaching in their synagogues, preaching the good news of the kingdom, and healing every disease and sickness among the people. News about him spread all over Syria, and people brought to him all who were ill with various diseases, those suffering severe pain, the demon- possessed, those having seizures, and the paralyzed, and he healed them."

Matthew 4:23-24

Prayer For Today

Heavenly Father, I thank You for Your powerful Word. Thank You for providing me with a Bible so that I can learn about Your ways and grow in a deeper understanding of who You are. Help me to believe Your Word and to apply it to my life all the days of my life. Your Word declares that You are the same yesterday, today and forevermore (Hebrews 13:8) and I can trust that what You have done before, you will do again, and that You will do it in my life. Thank You, Lord, for showing me in Your word that You healed all types of sicknesses and diseases. Thank You, Lord, for healing all who came to You. Dear Lord, I come to You with my illness (*describe it in your prayer*) and I humbly ask You, in the name of Jesus to heal my body from every pain, discomfort and disease. All these things I pray in the name of Jesus.

Amen.

The Body Of Christ –
God's Powerful Gift

We Need the Prayers of Others

"Is any one of you sick? He should call the elders of the church to pray over him and anoint him with oil in the name of the Lord. And the prayer offered in faith will make the sick person well; the Lord will raise him up. If he has sinned, he will be forgiven. Therefore confess your sins to each other and pray for each other so that you may be healed. The prayer of a righteous man is powerful and effective."

JAMES 5:14-16

"Dear friend, I pray that you may enjoy good health and that all may go well with you, even as your soul is getting along well."

3 JOHN 2

ONE OF MY FAVORITE PRAISE and worship songs is 'Think About His Love' by Don Moen. Take a look at what the chorus says:

Think about His love, think about His goodness
Think about His grace that's brought us through
For as high as the heavens above

So great is the measure of our Father's love
Great is the measure of our Father's love. So
great is the measure of our Father's love.

Every time I hear this song, I am reminded of the unfailing love of God. In His love He sent His Son, Jesus, to suffer and die on a cross so that we could be rescued from eternal damnation. Jesus was raised from the dead and He lives. He continually shows His immeasurable love for us, daily showering us with His many mercies. One way in which this is expressed is through His concern for every aspect of our lives. Take a look at what the Bible says:

"Cast all your anxiety on him because he cares for you"
1 Peter 5:7

The Lord cares for our physical bodies, our intellect, our personalities, our soul and our spirit. We can therefore bring all our concerns to Him, being fully assured that He will listen to us from a caring heart and respond in accordance with what is best for us.

In light of the Lord's concern for us, He lovingly instructs us to take specific steps when we are sick. The first instruction He gives us is to call for the elders of the church to pray over us and anoint us with oil in the name of the Lord (James 5:14). Nothing is wrong with praying for ourselves, but that is not the Lord's first instruction. There is also nothing wrong for us to seek medical help, but even that was not the first instruction from the Lord to us. The first instruction from the Lord, in the event that we are sick, is to call for the elders of the church.

One of the greatest gifts the Lord has given to us is the body of Christ – the Church. However, we are more likely to experience the spiritual gifts present in the Church if we are believers who are church-going as well as church-committed members. The norm for too many professing Christians is to be unattached to a local assembly and the negative result of this uncommitted behavior is that when trouble or sickness arises or occurs in their life they have no one to whom they can turn. If you have backslidden or you are not committed to a Bible teaching church, please return to the Lord quickly and fix that. The local assembly has been given to us for good reason and we NEED the Church – the body of believers.

Within every Bible-teaching church there are elders or leaders. Generally, these are mature, godly and blameless individuals who walk in obedience to the Word of God (Titus 1:6-7). The Lord has placed these godly leaders in His house to play a significant role in our spiritual well-being. When we call for the elders, we are not only walking in obedience to God's Word, but we are also exercising our faith in the Lord's ability to heal us.

The elder's role is to pray in faith for the sick person and anoint him/her with oil in the name of the Lord. It is the Lord who heals, but He often works through the prayers of His people. This is why we must never underestimate our desperate need for the prayers of godly believers. The Word of God tells us that the prayers of a righteous man are powerful and effective (James 5:16).

Of note also, in the above Scripture reference is the fact that God's Word tells us to confess our sins one to another and also pray for each other so that we may be healed (James 5:16). When we fall short in any way, it is essential for us to confess our sins to other godly believers. So often I speak with individuals who are fearful of confessing their sins to other godly believers, and instead choose to conceal their sin while praying for God's healing. Do not make that error. Obedience to the Word of the Lord opens the door for God's abundant blessings in our life. When we confess our sins to other godly believers, something very important occurs. We open the door for others to pray for us and, in turn, we receive God's healing touch in our lives.

Remember:
The local assembly has been given to us for good reason and we NEED the Church – the body of believers.

Challenge:
Memorize James 5:14-16
"Is any one of you sick? He should call the elders of the church to pray over him and anoint him with oil in the name of the Lord. And the prayer offered in faith will make the sick person well; the Lord will raise him up. If he has sinned, he will be forgiven. Therefore confess your sins to each other and pray for each other so that you may be healed. The prayer of a righteous man is powerful and effective."

Prayer For Today

Heavenly Father, I thank You for placing me among a family of believers – the body of Christ. Thank You for demonstrating Your great mercies towards me. You have not left me all alone in this walk but, You have blessed me with a company of believers. I thank You, Lord. Lord, help me not to keep my struggles and issues to myself, but to speak to others within the body of Christ. I confess that sometimes I have allowed fear to direct my life, but no longer, Lord. I want to be directed by Your Word and I want my life to be led by Your Holy Spirit, not by my thoughts. So today, Lord, I stand on the authority of Your Word. I ask You to help me to open up to my fellow believers and as I pray to You, Lord, I ask You to heal me of every sickness in my body. All these things I pray in the matchless name of Jesus.

Amen.

Your Healing Is Not Just For You

"As Peter traveled about the country, he went to visit the saints in Lydda. There he found a man named Aeneas, a paralytic who had been bedridden for eight years. "Aeneas," Peter said to him, "Jesus Christ heals you. Get up and take care of your mat." Immediately Aeneas got up. All those who lived in Lydda and Sharon saw him and turned to the Lord."

ACTS 9:32-35

"Stretch out your hand to heal and perform miraculous signs and wonders through the name of your holy servant Jesus."

ACTS 4:30

AS BELIEVERS IN CHRIST, ONE temptation we face, almost daily, is to exalt what we see above the power of our Lord. Our adversary, Satan, is always trying to make God appear small in our eyes, and our problems, like gigantic mountains. As a master deceiver, he continually uses trickery to rob us of God's eternal promises. This is why it is imperative for us to keep our faces in the Word of God, and train our minds to exalt God's Word above the devil's lies.

As we continue in our journey towards God's divine healing in our lives, we must ensure that we do not, in any way, place a limit on the power of God. Regardless of how much pain you are currently experiencing, or the devastating news you have heard from doctors, faithfully seek the Lord's voice with a believing heart. God has lovingly blessed us with His Word, and our final conclusion on any matter must always be based on what God has said in His Word. Never allow yourself to get in the habit of exalting anyone's story, even your own, above the Word of God.

Nothing is impossible for the Lord. Absolutely nothing! By casually reading God's Word, we repeatedly see the miraculous hand of the Lord working in the midst of humanly impossible situations, and guess what? God's power is available to us today as well. It was not just for the good old days. In today's devotion, we are going to study the life of Aeneas to see the awesome power of the Lord at work. My prayer is that you will experience His mighty hand in your present situation.

Aeneas was a man who had been paralyzed and was bedridden for eight years. Imagine that, if you will, for a moment! This man, who once knew what it was like to walk, run, sit and stand became physically disabled. For all of eight years, he could do nothing for himself. Someone had to feed him, bathe him, and help him to use the bathroom. If he wanted to scratch somewhere on his body, he needed someone's help.

It is not unusual, in such unfavorable situations to adjust our lives and sometimes, even our faith in order to accommodate our present predicament. It is not easy to have a biblical or hopeful view of life when we have a painful pill to swallow. However, in the midst of it all, we must remember that our Savior is always up to something good. We might not understand what we are going through, but we must faithfully grow in the conviction that all things are working together for the good of those who love the Lord and are called according to His purpose (Romans 8:28).

As bad as things were in the life of Aeneas, God was at work through the ministry of His servant Peter. Amazingly, the apostle Peter was busy ministering in Lydda, the town where Aeneas resided, and he was led to come in contact with Aeneas.

Personally, I love this account in God's Word because it shows the great love and interest the Lord has for every single one of us! Aeneas could not move around to find Peter, but the Lord allowed the apostle Peter to find Aeneas. That is amazing! It had been eight long years, but the Lord had not forgotten Aeneas. In the same manner, the Lord has not forgotten you! Regardless of how long you have suffered with your present illness or disability, it is so important to remember this truth – **The Lord has not forgotten you**.

The apostle Peter, operating under the leadership of the Holy Spirit said: "Aeneas, Jesus Christ heals you..." (Acts 9:34), and he was healed. Please do not miss this. It is not some mighty evangelist who heals – only Jesus heals! The apostle Peter was the vessel, but the Healer is Jesus. Never forget that! Jesus healed in the days of the apostle Peter and He still heals today. Look at what the Bible says: "Jesus Christ is the same yesterday and today and forever" (Hebrews 13:8). If Jesus healed yesterday, He will heal today. There is no sickness, illness, disability or physical problem that Jesus will not heal.

Before closing this chapter, it is important to point out Acts 9:35 which states:

> "All those who lived in Lydda and Sharon
> saw him and turned to the Lord".

Jesus wants more for us than mere healing. He wants people to put their trust in Him. That is exactly what happened when unbelievers saw Aeneas. They knew of his former condition. For eight years, everyone in the town of Lydda saw him as a helpless bedridden man. However, they now saw that a miracle had occurred in his life. Aeneas' healing was not just for himself, it also served as a way of helping those in Lydda and Sharon to turn to the Healer, Jesus.

When the Lord heals you, make sure you testify about the mighty healing hand of the Lord. See to it that you give all the credit and the glory to God. Your sickness might be personal but God's deliverance is not. The Lord wants people to know who He is and sometimes He allows everyone to see you sick so that when He heals you, everyone will know and understand the power of the Savior. Never let your healing be a secret. Boldly declare what the Lord has done for you to an unbelieving world and sometimes, to an unbelieving church, as your testimony will help someone put their trust in Jesus.

Remember:
The Lord has not forgotten you.

Challenge:
Memorize Acts 9:34

> "Aeneas," Peter said to him, "Jesus Christ heals you. Get up and take care of your mat." Immediately Aeneas got up."
>
> Acts 9:34

PRAYER FOR TODAY

Heavenly Father, I thank You for Your great grace extended towards me. Forgive me, Lord, for the times I have struggled to believe You. Thank You, Lord, for not forgetting me. Thank You, Lord, for Your continued encouragement in my life to hold on to Your Word above every other voice in my life. As You work mightily in my life, Lord, help me to remember to give all the credit to You. You are the Great Healer and I give all the glory to You, Lord. There is no name above Your name, Lord, and there is no power greater than Yours. You hold all authority over every sickness and disease and Lord, I look to You and You alone for my healing. Thank You, Lord, for always coming to me and strengthening me. I will continue to look to You with eager expectation. All these things I pray in the name of Jesus.

Amen.

Will God Heal When It Was My Fault?

Why Did I Do That?

"When Jesus' followers saw what was going to happen,
they said, "Lord, should we strike with our swords?" And
one of them struck the servant of the high priest, cutting
off his right ear. But Jesus answered, "No more of this!"
And he touched the man's ear and healed him."

LUKE 22:49-51

HAVE YOU EVER FELT AS if you were just in the wrong place, at the wrong time? I am sure you know that deep feeling of regret. You replay the story in your head a million times asking yourself, "Why did I go there?" What tends to produce even more guilt, is if you ended up suffering physical harm, and the after-effects are still present in your life today.

In one form or another, I have been asked this guilt-filled question: "Will God heal me, when it is my own fault?" Let us take a look at the Word of God to find out the answer to this question.

In Luke 22:47-51, there is a rather interesting sequence of events. Jesus was betrayed by Judas, one of His own disciples, and a band of soldiers had come to arrest Him. One of Jesus' zealous followers wanted to protect the Lord from any harm and he asked: "Lord, should we strike with our swords?"(Luke 22:49). Before Jesus responded, this overly zealous follower of Christ drew his sword and struck the servant of the high priest, cutting off his right ear (Luke 22:50).

Imagine for a moment, how this servant must have felt! Not only was he in great physical pain, but he was now faced with the prospect of having to live without an ear, and with great guilt for the rest of his life. After all, why was he persecuting Jesus? Someone who had done absolutely no wrong to him. Why was he such a willing participant to such an evil scheme – that of hurting the Creator of the world? Surely he should live without an ear to remind him of his evil and malicious deed all the days of his life. Although this is how many of us would think, we can be forever grateful that God is not like us. His ways are certainly not similar to our ways and His thoughts are far different from our own (Isaiah 55:8).

Psalm 103:10 beautifully declares:

"He does not treat us as our sins deserve or repay us according to our iniquities."

Although our own thoughts can condemn us, we have to learn to exalt what God has said about Himself above what we think we deserve. The Lord has made it clear that He does not treat us as our sins deserve. Thank you, Lord!

The servant whose ear was damaged did not even ask Jesus to help him. Maybe, he was too overwhelmed with pain to think about that, or probably, he felt unworthy to ask for help – whatever the case may have been, Jesus did something rather loving and merciful. He first rebuked His overly zealous follower and reached out and touched the man's ear and healed him (Luke 22:51).

Think about that for a minute! This man came to harm the Lord and he instead ended up being harmed. And the same Lord he came to harm was the one who healed his bleeding ear. This is a powerful example of how great the Lord's mercy is to us! Never allow guilty feelings to coerce you to see the Lord as One who is vindictive. With utter sincerity, look at who the Lord is, from His Word. Forget about who you are and boldly approach the throne of grace in your time of need and humbly ask the Lord to heal you.

The Lord heals us not because of who we are, but in light of who He is. Take him at His Word and rest all your confidence in who He is and receive your healing in Jesus' name.

Remember:
The Lord does not treat us as our sins deserve or repay us according to our iniquities (Psalm 103:10).

Challenge:
Memorize Psalm 103:10

> "He does not treat us as our sins deserve or repay us according to our iniquities"
>
> Psalm 103:10

PRAYER FOR TODAY

Heavenly Father, I thank You for Your compassion, mercy and loving-kindness towards me. So often, I have been tempted to think that You are out to get me and treat me as I deserve. However, Lord, I thank You for Your great grace towards me in the name of Jesus. I thank You for not treating me as my sins deserve. I thank You for Your loving hand towards me. Indeed, I can look to You at all times and I can expect Your great grace to be extended towards me because of who You are. Again, I thank You, Lord, for Your loving-kindness towards me. In Jesus' name I pray.

Amen.

Jesus Heals All Types Of Sicknesses

Jesus Heals Deformities

"Going on from that place, he went into their synagogue, and
a man with a shriveled hand was there. Looking for a reason
to accuse Jesus, they asked him, "Is it lawful to heal on the
Sabbath?" He said to them, "If any of you has a sheep and it
falls into a pit on the Sabbath, will you not take hold of it and
lift it out? How much more valuable is a man than a sheep!
Therefore it is lawful to do good on the Sabbath." Then he
said to the man, "Stretch out your hand." So he stretched it out
and it was completely restored, just as sound as the other."

MATTHEW 12:9-13

"Jesus Christ is the same yesterday and today and forever."

HEBREWS 13:8

IT IS REALLY UNFORTUNATE THAT there are many professing Christians who
are against healing, and who actively seek to persuade us to believe the
erroneous view that the Lord will not bring healing to our lives today.
These self-professed scholars openly exalt their academic and intellec-
tual limitations above the Word of God, claiming that miracles and healing were for the days of old and not for the New Testament Church
Christian.

Although acts of God's healing power are littered throughout the Bible, there are pastoral leaders who are more in love with their theological persuasions than with the Word of God, and, because of this, there is a fight against the healing power of the Lord in many local assemblies.

In Jesus' time on earth, there were some scholars known as the Pharisees who, by exalting their ideological doctrines above God's Word, tried to deny people from experiencing God's healing power. One such doctrine was that no healing should be done on the Sabbath day. Let us take a closer look at the account in the reference above.

On one occasion, there was a man in the synagogue who had a physical handicap – his hand was shriveled. Instead of being filled with compassion for this man, the Pharisees were more concerned with the doctrines surrounding the Sabbath day, and they exalted their doctrines to such an extent that they were utterly insensitive to the move of God that was about to take place in their midst. Unfortunately, there are leaders just like the Pharisees in the church today, who, by their unscriptural teachings, are preventing believers from receiving God's Word on healing, and are also stifling God's healing power.

Thankfully, Jesus was not dissuaded by the traditions of the Pharisees. He saw through their hypocrisy and asked them a personal question regarding their own cattle, about which they seemed to be deeply concerned. Take a look at what Jesus said:

> "If any of you has a sheep and it falls into a pit on the Sabbath, will you not take hold of it and lift it out?"
>
> Matthew 12:11

Amazingly, the same Pharisees who were not open to anyone being healed on the Sabbath, were very open to saving their own animals on the Sabbath. Wow! Shamefully, they placed greater importance on helping their own animals than on helping a disabled human being receive healing from the Lord. Jesus had to graciously remind them that a man was of far more worth than a sheep (Mathew 12:12).

Throughout God's Word we are faithfully reminded that the Lord loves each and every one of us, and that He cares so much for us. Although this disabled man was being overlooked by the religious system of the day, Jesus would not stand for it. In front of the Pharisees Jesus said to the man:

"Stretch out your hand"

Matthew 12:13

Thankfully, he obeyed the instruction of the Lord. He did not allow himself to become overwhelmed with intimidation because of the presence of the Pharisees. Neither did he allow the false teaching of the Pharisees to influence him and rob him of being healed at that moment. In spite of all the unbelievers around him, he obeyed the Lord, stretched out his hand and he was healed.

Whatever the Word of God says about healing, just believe it and obey it. Never allow the 'Pharisees' to intimidate you and prevent you from walking in obedience to the Word of the Lord. If you were to ask the man in Mathew 12 if Jesus heals, he would answer with a resounding, 'Yes'.

Do you have a body part that needs to be completely restored? Look to Jesus, the One who heals. He is the same yesterday, today and forevermore (Hebrews 13:8).

Remember:
Whatever the Word of God says about healing, just believe it and obey it.

Challenge:
Memorize Hebrews 13:8

"Jesus Christ is the same yesterday and today and forever."

Hebrews 13:8

PRAYER FOR TODAY

Heavenly Father, I thank You that my healing does not depend on what others think, but on what You have said in Your Word. I thank You for reminding me that You are the same yesterday, today and forever. I thank You for what You did yesterday, because I can trust that You will do the same thing today, and I also trust that You will do the same thing again and again. You are the Great Healer and I humbly look to You to conform everything in me to your immeasurable will. All these things I pray in the name of Jesus.

Amen.

Jesus Heals Blind Eyes

"As Jesus went on from there, two blind men followed
him, calling out, "Have mercy on us, Son of David!"
When he had gone indoors, the blind men came to
him, and he asked them, "Do you believe that I am able
to do this?" "Yes, Lord," they replied. Then he touched
their eyes and said, "According to your faith will it
be done to you"; and their sight was restored...."

MATTHEW 9:27-30A

THERE IS IMMENSE VALUE IN seeking the Lord. Just take a look at what
Hebrews 11:6 says:

"And without faith it is impossible to please God, because anyone who comes to him must believe that he exists and that he
rewards those who earnestly seek him."

Hebrews 11:6

As long as the aim of our seeking is the Lord Himself, we can rest assured
that our seeking will never be a futile endeavor. Psalm 25:3 declares:

"No one whose hope is in you will ever be put to shame..."

In this chapter, we are going to learn from two blind men who understood this truth and pursued Jesus with all their heart and were healed.

In today's Scripture reference, we read about two unnamed blind men who followed Jesus and called out to him, saying:

> "Have mercy on us, Son of David!"
>
> Matthew 9:27b

Already, this true account seems very fascinating. Imagine, for a moment, the two blind men. How were they able to follow Jesus? Was someone leading them? Were they receiving some sort of guidance in order to keep up with the Lord? The text does not tell us how they managed to follow the Lord, but we are told that they did. They were so desperate to receive the healing touch of Jesus they overcame every obstacle in their way in order to remain within reach of the Lord Jesus.

There are some people who want to be healed, but they do not make any effort to pursue Jesus. They refuse to go to Church and ask the elders to anoint them and pray for them; they refuse to seek out godly Christian leaders and ask them to pray for them; they do not read or study the Word of God on healing. Amazingly they do not make any effort to seek the Lord for their own healing. This was certainly not the perspective of these two blind men. They made every effort to pursue Jesus for their healing, and so must we.

In their pursuit of Jesus, the Healer, they kept crying out:

> "Have mercy on us, Son of David!"
>
> Matthew 9:27

What does this mean for us today? It means that we continually pray for our healing. We cry out in prayer to our Lord and Savior until he hears us and heals us. Do not just hope to be healed, cry out for your healing! Jesus hears our cry and He answers us when we call upon His name.

As they cried out to Jesus, He responded with a question:

"Do you believe that I am able to do this?"

Matthew 9:28

We all have to deal with this question personally. At times, if we are being honest, we would have to admit that we believe that Jesus is capable of healing us, but we do not think He is going to do it for us. Why do we doubt that Jesus is able and willing to heal us? One of the reasons, I believe, is that we struggle to accept that Jesus is the same today as He is revealed in the Word of God. He is still the Great Healer, just as He was in the days of old. He still has the power to heal every disease, sickness, pain and deformity as revealed in the Scriptures.

The blind men answered Jesus' question with a resounding: 'Yes, Lord' (Matthew 9:28b). After they expressed their belief, Jesus touched their eyes and made a remarkable statement:

"According to your faith will it be done to you"

Matthew 9:29b

Our faith, that is, our belief in Jesus plays a powerful role in what we receive from the Lord. These blind men wholeheartedly looked to Jesus for healing and they were rewarded with the very healing they sought.

Throughout the Scriptures we see Jesus emphasizing the importance of our faith, and this faith comes as we immerse ourselves in God's Word (Romans 10:17). May your faith in Jesus continually increase as you immerse yourself in the Word of God, and may He open your eyes to see Him as He is revealed therein.

One final thought, as it relates to these two blind men. Did you notice that there were two of them? It seems so obvious, I know, but it is very important. Not only did these two men have the company of each other, they also had agreement with each other. They were united in their minds, in their pursuit, and also in their prayers to Jesus. Agreement is essential! Look at what the Bible says:

> "Again, I tell you that if two of you on earth agree about anything you ask for, it will be done for you by my Father in heaven. For where two or three come together in my name, there am I with them."
>
> Matthew 18:19-20

We should always be thankful to the Lord for the body of Christ. In His wisdom, the Lord has blessed us with godly brothers and sisters in Christ, and we must ask them to cry out with us to the Lord for the healing we so desperately need.

Remember:
These blind men wholeheartedly looked to Jesus for healing and they were rewarded with the very healing they sought.

Challenge:
Memorize Hebrews 11:6

> "And without faith it is impossible to please God, because anyone who comes to him must believe that he exists and that he rewards those who earnestly seek him."
>
> Hebrews 11:6

PRAYER FOR TODAY

Heavenly Father, I thank You for Your Word. Dear Lord, You have said in Your Word: "Come near to God and he will come near to you" (James 4:8). Today, I draw near to You, Lord, with all of my heart and I thank You for drawing near to me. Thank You, Lord, for strengthening me to pursue You. Today, Lord, I want to pursue You with wholehearted devotion. I give up all that I desire and ask You to fill me with a sincere desire to pursue You with all of my heart. I just want to seek You, Lord, because of who You are and not because of what I want from You. I want to pursue You, Lord, with a pure heart. All these things I pray in the name of Jesus.

Amen.

Jesus Heals Skin Diseases

"Naaman's servant went to him and said, "My father, if the
prophet had told you to do some great thing, would you not
have done it? How much more, then, when he tells you, 'Wash
and be cleansed'!" So he went down and dipped himself in the
Jordan seven times, as the man of God had told him, and his
flesh was restored and became clean like that of a young boy."

2 Kings 5:13-14

"He sent forth his word and healed them;
he rescued them from the grave."

Psalm 107:20

ARE YOU AWARE THAT YOU might be blocking the very healing for which you
are hoping? In order to gain insight into this point, let us take a look at
the life of Naaman, an outstanding Aramean soldier.

Naaman was the commander of the army of Aram and was greatly
respected by its king, because through him, the Lord had bestowed
many victories on their land (2 Kings 5:1). There was, however, something wrong with Naaman – he had a debilitating disease called leprosy.

It happened that a young Israelite girl who had been taken captive
by Aramean soldiers ended up serving Naaman's wife (2 Kings 5:2). This

young woman knew that the power of God was available to heal Naaman, so she said to her mistress:

> "If only my master (Naaman) would see the prophet who is in Samaria! He would cure him of his leprosy."
>
> 2 Kings 5:3

Naaman responded to the good news he had received and requested the approval of the king of Aram to go to Samaria to visit Elisha, the mighty man of God. What happened next is very important!

When Naaman arrived at Elisha's house, Elisha did not go out to meet him. Instead, he sent one of his servants to tell Naaman that he had to go and wash seven times in the Jordan in order to be healed (2 Kings 5:9-10). This approach by Elisha did not sit well with Naaman at all. He became very angry and said:

> "I thought that he would surely come out to me and stand and call on the name of the Lord his God, wave his hand over the spot and cure me of leprosy. Are not Abana and Pharpar, the rivers of Damascus, better than any of the waters of Israel? Couldn't I wash in them and be cleansed?" So he turned and went off in a rage."
>
> 2 Kings 5:11-12

Naaman's response gives us at least three 'enemies' that can keep us from being healed. Let us take a look at each of them!

THREE ENEMIES OF HEALING
The First Enemy - Your Own Thoughts
The first two words that left Naaman's mouth were 'I thought'. Naaman went to Samaria to see the prophet Elisha in order to be healed and he received an instruction that would bring healing to his body. In his

own mind, however, he had thoughts about the process by which he was to be healed. When the prophet's procedure was not in accordance with his thoughts, he became angry and rejected the very cure for his sickness.

Naaman almost missed his healing because he exalted his own thoughts above the Word of God which was declared through the prophet, Elisha, the Lord's manservant. Like Naaman, we also can place our own thoughts above God's Word and end up missing the healing that we so desperately desire. We are never going to think along the same lines as the Lord. His wisdom far exceeds our own, and His ways are not our ways. Take a look at what the Bible says:

> ""For my thoughts are not your thoughts, neither are your ways my ways," declares the Lord"
>
> Isaiah 55:8

When the Lord gives us an instruction, our only response should be: 'Yes, Lord'.

The Second Enemy – Your Own Way

The second enemy that almost robbed Naaman from being healed was his own way. He had a preference for how the healing should take place. Look at what he said:

> "I thought that he would surely come out to me and stand and call on the name of the Lord his God, wave his hand over the spot and cure me of my leprosy."
>
> 2 Kings 5:11

Naaman had a particular procedure in his mind of how Elisha should have operated. He expected Elisha to greet him, stand before him, call upon the Lord for him, wave his hand over his sick body and heal him. When Elisha did not do the things he had expected, he was indignant.

As believers, we can behave like Naaman. We can be expecting a miraculous healing, but the Lord has given a simple instruction through the doctors, and we reject it because we want a miraculous or flamboyant intervention by the Lord. We must always remember that the Lord's ways are not our ways (Isaiah 55:8). There are times He will heal supernaturally, but there are times he will heal through the advice of medical doctors. Either way, it is the Lord who brings the healing.

The Third Enemy – Your Own Emotions
Naaman was told to go and dip seven times in the Jordan in order to be healed (2 Kings 5:10), but because his predetermined expectations were not met, he became angry and refused to obey the Word of the Lord through the prophet Elisha. Imagine that! He had heard the very answer that would bring healing to his body, but instead of being filled with gratitude, he was filled with anger. He was so angry that he was willing to go back home sick.

Being angry at God's Word carries absolutely zero benefit for us. In anger, Naaman was about to make a decision to live with a debilitating disease for the rest of his life. He had travelled so many miles to receive the healing touch of the Lord, but was about to let his emotions rob him of the opportunity to be completely healed.

Never get angry at God's Word. His Word has been given to us for our own good. If the Holy Spirit reminds you of the Word of God which instructs you to forgive someone who has offended you, do not be angry, instead, forgive the person. It could very well be that your healing is linked to your forgiveness, and instead of walking in the healing God has provided, you are walking around sick and angry like Naaman. Our emotions must never be exalted above God's Word. The answer that God gives may not be pleasing to your ears, but it will bring health to your body.

So how did Naaman get healed?
Fortunately for Naaman, he eventually listened to his servants who were with him. They reasoned with him saying:

"My father, if the prophet had told you to do some great thing, would you not have done it? How much more, then, when he tells you, 'Wash and be cleansed'!"

2 Kings 5:13

Thankfully, Naaman listened to his wise servants. He humbled himself and submitted to the Word of the Lord. He threw off his own beliefs, emotions, thoughts and reasoning, obeyed the Word of God by dipping seven times in the Jordan, and, guess what? He was completely healed!

The more you study the Word of God, you will find that healing is deeply connected to the obedience of God's Word. May we always embrace the Word of the Lord and experience His mighty healing power in our lives.

Remember:
He humbled himself and submitted to the Word of the Lord. He threw off his own beliefs, emotions, thoughts and reasoning, obeyed the Word of God by dipping seven times in the Jordan, and, guess what? He was completely healed!

Challenge: Memorize

"He sent forth his word and healed them; he rescued them from the grave."

Psalm 107:20

Prayer For Today

Heavenly Father, I thank You for providing me with an answer to my situation. Help me never to reject Your answer because it was not what I expected to hear. Help me, Lord, to increasingly recognize that You are perfect and good and all that You do is perfect and good. Today, Lord,

I acknowledge my lowly state before You. Your ways and Your thoughts are higher than my own, and I humbly submit to You. I place my trust in You, Lord, and I thank You for all that You have done in my life so far. All these things I pray in the name of Jesus.

Amen.

Desperate Faith

"He said to her, "Daughter, your faith has healed you.
Go in peace and be freed from your suffering.""

MARK 5:34

"And without faith it is impossible to please God, because
anyone who comes to him must believe that he exists
and that he rewards those who earnestly seek him."

HEBREWS 11:6

WE ALL ARE LIKELY FAMILIAR with the Biblical account of the woman with the issue of blood. Should you be unaware of her story, please read Mark 5. This unnamed woman had been plagued by a serious illness for twelve long years (Mark 5:25), but she eventually experienced the healing power of Jesus in her life in a tremendous way.

In this chapter, we are going to look at five powerful lessons that we can learn from her life. Let us jump right into it!

Our First Lesson – She Never Lost Hope of Being Healed

One of the first lessons we can learn from this woman who was sick for a number of years, is that she did not sit down and have a pity party. She was always hopeful that she would be healed, and she actively sought help from many doctors, spending everything she had in the hope of getting better. This is a rather valuable lesson for us because it is not unusual for one to be deeply discouraged if healing takes a long time.

Although this woman's healing came after twelve gruesome years, she was filled with hope during the waiting period! May the Lord use her story to encourage us as we wait for His healing touch in our own lives.

Our Second Lesson – She Constantly Sought Help

There is a wonderful sequence that the Lord has given us. He says:

> "Ask and you shall receive, seek and you shall find, knock and the door will be opened unto you."
>
> Matthew 7:7

In her sickness, this unnamed woman faithfully kept asking for help. The Bible says:

> "She had suffered a great deal under the care of many doctors."
>
> Mark 5:26

This shows that she had gone to several physicians looking for a cure for her illness.

We have to learn to keep looking for the answer to the problems we face, instead of quickly assuming that a solution does not exist. Look and keep looking! Faithfully search for the answer to your sickness in the Word of God, because the answer is there. This woman asked MANY doctors. If one doctor told her that she could not be cured, she chose to see the incompetence of the doctor and not the impossibility of her healing. She would go from clinic to clinic searching for the answer to her problem because she was determined not to live with this sickness in her life.

Our Third Lesson – She Did Not Allow the Crowd To Deter Her
The third lesson, which is perhaps one of the most important for us to bear in mind, is that this woman did not allow any obstacles to prevent her from touching Jesus. The Bible tells us that there was a crowd around Jesus (Mark 5:27), and that could have discouraged her from getting close to the Lord. However, in spite of the large number of people, this woman made up her mind that she was not going to let anyone stop her from touching the Lord. If she had to push, shove and lift people out of her way, she was going to do it, if that was what it would take to make contact with Jesus.

For us to walk in the healing power of the Lord, we have to learn not to let anything block us from making contact with the presence of the Lord. We have to be willing to go through whatever we need to in order to receive our healing from the Lord.

Our Fourth Lesson – She encouraged herself
No one could understand what this lady was going through. She had no one to give her words of encouragement, but she was not deterred; she simply encouraged herself. Take a look at what she said:

"If I just touch his clothes, I will be healed."

Mark 5:28

She encouraged herself to make contact with Jesus. In the same way, in our sick state, we have to encourage ourselves in the Lord. We will not always have someone saying the right words to us, but we can certainly say the right Biblical words to ourselves.

Our Fifth Lesson – She Touched Jesus
Contact with Jesus is what we all need, but how do we get it? Through faith! Let me explain.

When the woman touched Jesus with the intention of being healed, the Bible tells us that Jesus asked the crowd: "Who touched my clothes?"

The question confounded the disciples because they were so many people present. However, the lady, knowing what she had done, came forward and confessed that she had touched the Lord. Jesus' response to her should not be overlooked:

> "Daughter, your faith has healed you. Go in peace and be freed from your suffering."
>
> Mark 5:34

The healing came as a result of her faith in Jesus. That is the type of faith we need. Faith that moves us out of our comfort zone to approach the Lord and experience His mighty healing touch.

My prayer for you is that your faith will increase and that you will draw near to the Lord and make contact with Him through prayer today.

Remember:
If she had to push, shove and lift people out of her way, she was going to do it, if that was what it would take to make contact with Jesus.

Challenge:
Memorize Mark 5:34 and Hebrews 11:6

> "He said to her, "Daughter, your faith has healed you. Go in peace and be freed from your suffering.""
>
> Mark 5:34

> "And without faith it is impossible to please God, because anyone who comes to him must believe that he exists and that he rewards those who earnestly seek him."
>
> Hebrews 11:6

PRAYER FOR TODAY

Heavenly Father, I thank You for Your love and for Your mercy towards me. I thank You for encouraging me to seek Your face. This woman, who had the issue of blood, encountered numerous disappointments when she sought the help of medical doctors, but the first time she sought help from You – the Great Physician, You healed her. It is never a waste of time to come to You, Lord. You are my Healer, and I look to You, Jesus, for healing. Thank You, Lord, for touching my life. Even now, Lord, I receive Your healing in my body in the mighty name of Jesus. Thank You, Lord. In Jesus' name I pray.

Amen.

Pain, Suffering
and Demons

DAY 11

Be Free! In Jesus' Name

"On a Sabbath Jesus was teaching in one of the synagogues,
and a woman was there who had been crippled by a
spirit for eighteen years. She was bent over and could
not straighten up at all. When Jesus saw her, he called
her forward and said to her, "Woman, you are set free
from your infirmity." Then he put his hands on her, and
immediately she straightened up and praised God."

LUKE 13:10-13

"The first step on the way to victory is to recognize the enemy."

CORRIE TEN BOOM

IT IS IMPORTANT TO HAVE a balanced view and not to assume that every disease is of satanic origin. However, as believers in Christ, we cannot afford to overlook the fact that some sicknesses come directly from the devil himself. In this section of the book, we will look at a few examples of diseases caused by Satan and his horde of demons, and we shall also see that the power of God is able to deliver and heal all who have suffered from satanic oppression.

In Luke 13:10-17, we read about a woman who had been severely crippled for eighteen years – quite a long time! Her crippled state kept her in a bent position, and she could not straighten up at all (Luke 13:11). The Word of God wastes no time with speculations, but instead makes it clear that a demonic spirit was responsible for her condition. There was no cure in the natural, and no amount of medication would have helped her, because her disability was a direct result of a demonic agent. Think about that for a moment! For eighteen long years, this demonic spirit had made this lady's body its home and had kept her crippled, not loosening its diabolical grip for one moment!

Let us see how she was finally set free from this awful condition. Luke 13:10-11(a) has a lot of information and we cannot afford to disregard the wisdom found in these few verses:

"On a Sabbath Jesus was teaching in one of the synagogues, and a woman was there who had been crippled by a spirit for eighteen years. She was bent over and could not straighten up at all."

Luke 13:10-11

As we seek the Lord for our healing we must never underestimate the value of any word in the Bible. Every single word has divine authority to help us walk in the healing power of God. There are four main points that we can take from these few verses of Scripture.

1. The Woman's Crippled State Did Not Prevent Her From Going To The House of The Lord

Although this unidentified crippled woman was physically incapacitated for eighteen years, we are told that she was in the synagogue. How amazing! Here was someone who had many reasons not to go to the synagogue. She could have argued that she was uncomfortable, or that people might look at her and make her feel ashamed. She could have reasoned to herself that she had been going there for a long time, and her condition had not changed. She had very good reasons not to be in the synagogue, but the Bible tells us that she was there – crippled, bent over, uncomfortable, in pain, but present.

Too often we can allow our illness to dictate whether or not we show up at our 'synagogue' – church. Unfortunately, the church is the last place some people expect to meet the Lord, and many end up missing the move of God because they allow their suffering to keep them away from the place where Jesus will be. In no way am I suggesting that Jesus cannot show up wherever you are, because He definitely can, but we must never underestimate the fact that Jesus always shows up when His people gather in His name to meet Him. This woman teaches us that our physical handicaps are not excuses for avoiding the house of the Lord.

2. A Long Time Does Not Mean The Lord Has Forgotten You

From this brief passage of scripture, we also learn that while the woman's illness lasted for eighteen years, the Lord had not forgotten her. She may have gone to the synagogue time and time again without any encouraging signs that she would be healed, but that did not mean that the Lord was not going to heal her. Never forget that! A long time in a bad situation does not mean that the Lord wants us to remain in that position. You might be tempted to cope with your illness, but DON'T. We serve a living God who heals and delivers, and I encourage you to allow this anonymous woman's testimony to encourage you to keep this in mind – the Lord has not forgotten you! Weeping may endure for a night, but joy comes in the morning (Psalm 30:5).

3. She Was Present During The Teaching of The Word of God

Another point we cannot afford to overlook is that before this crippled woman was healed, she was present during the teaching of the Word of God (Luke 13:10-11). As she listened to God's powerful Word, being taught by our Lord Jesus Himself, the demonic spirit had no choice but to come into direct contact with the most powerful weapon capable of destroying its diabolical stronghold – the Word. This is exactly why we must never remove ourselves from under the preaching of the Word of God. As we continually expose ourselves to God's Word, demonic strongholds loosen their grip on our lives, and we are freed from Satan's evil activity.

4. Only Jesus Destroys Demonic Strongholds

Finally, only Jesus can destroy the strongholds in our lives set up by evil spirits. Please remember that this woman's condition was not grounded in the physical realm which could be treated medically. Her sickness originated in the spiritual realm. It was a demonic agent that was responsible for her debilitating condition, and only Jesus could set her free.

Although the devil would love for us to suffer endlessly under his oppressive forces, Jesus actively ensures that this does not happen. We can rest assured that the Lord will ALWAYS deliver His children from every satanic attack. Look at how the apostle John puts it:

"The reason the Son of God appeared was to destroy the devil's work."

1 John 3:8b

Jesus does not play around with the devil, instead, He destroys his work. It is crucial though, that we take special note of the sequence of events before the woman was set free. The Bible tells us that Jesus called her forward (Luke 13:12). She had to go to Jesus first. She had to respond to the call of the Lord. When He calls you, always respond to Him. If He calls you out of an unequally yoked relationship, respond to His call. If He is calling you out of a sexually impure relationship, respond to Him. If He calls you to surrender your life to Him, please respond. Too often, we want to be touched by Jesus but we do not want to respond in obedience to His call. This woman first responded in obedience to Jesus' call, and then she was set free from her sickness (Luke 13:12). Jesus placed his hands on her, and the Bible tells us that she straightened up and praised God. She was finally released from that evil spirit and its crippling effects. Praise the Lord!

Jesus is still in the business of liberating people from demonic agents, and the harm they inflict. Just as He set this woman free, He will likewise do the same for you. May Jesus set you free from every foul and oppressive spirit, in the name of Jesus!

Remember:

As we continually listen to the Word of God, demonic strongholds lose their grip on our lives, and we are freed from Satan's evil activity.

Challenge:
Memorize Acts 10:38

> "How God anointed Jesus of Nazareth with the Holy Spirit and power, and how he went around doing good and healing all who were under the power of the devil, because God was with him."

PRAYER FOR TODAY

Heavenly Father, I thank You for Your love and grace toward me. I am so glad that there is nothing that is too difficult for You. All demonic spirits have to bow at Your feet, and nothing can overpower You. In the mighty name of Jesus, I command every demonic spirit to leave my body, my mind and my soul. In Jesus' name, every spirit of oppression, depart from me. I thank You, Lord for Your mighty hand upon my life. Thank You, Lord, for setting me free. All these things I pray in the name of Jesus.

Amen.

A Mother's Desperate Cry

"Then Jesus answered, "Woman, you have
great faith! Your request is granted." And her
daughter was healed from that very hour."

MATTHEW 15:28

"Ask and it will be given to you; seek and you will
find; knock and the door will be opened to you. For
everyone who asks receives; he who seeks finds; and
to him who knocks, the door will be opened."

MATTHEW 7:7-8

EVERY PARENT IS AWARE OF the anxiety that can be felt when there is something wrong with one of their children. We are never comfortable knowing that they do not feel well, and if we could take the sickness upon ourselves in order to give relief to our little ones, we would surely do it.

In Matthew 15:22-28, there is a very interesting conversation that occurs between Jesus and a Canaanite woman. Her daughter was suffering a great deal because of a demon, and, like any normal mother, she desperately tried to find the best help she could. She therefore went to Jesus to plead with Him to heal her daughter, but He completely ignored her. Just imagine that for a moment! You plead with the Lord, the only one who can save your child from their terrible suffering, and Jesus says nothing, absolutely nothing. In one way or another, we have all experienced something like this. We pray to the Lord, and there is no response. We fast, and there is still no answer. We pray a little more, but there is only silence. Everything remains the same, and we urgently need the Lord to intervene – a very troubling state of affairs.

What do we do when we are desperate for the Lord to help us, and we cry out for His divine intervention, and there is no response? The temptation many of us face at this point is to stop praying. In our desperation for an immediate answer, we give up on the Lord and falsely conclude that His silence means 'no'.

This Canaanite woman did not hear a word from the Lord but she did something quite remarkable. She began harassing the Lord's disciples for their help, and they found it so troublesome that they begged Jesus to send her away (Matthew 15:23). Did you see that? This woman's constant cry for help caused the disciples to start talking to Jesus about her issue – albeit for a completely different reason.

We must always bear in mind that others can speak to the Lord on our behalf. That is exactly what the disciples did. Their request for the Lord to get rid of her played a significant role in directing the attention of the Lord to her. Something remarkable always occurs when others speak to the Lord on our behalf, even when those prayers were not specifically made to help us.

At first Jesus ignored her, but after the disciples spoke to Him, he responded to the mother, saying:

> "I was sent only to the lost sheep of Israel."
>
> Matthew 15:24

Wow! That was definitely not the answer she was hoping for. After hearing such a remark, most of us would have felt so humiliated that we would have walked away in hopelessness, but not this Canaanite woman.

Being desperate for a 'yes' from the Lord, she did not leave His presence. Despite all the ridicule she had experienced, she was undeterred and did the unthinkable – she worshipped Jesus. The Bible tells us that she knelt before Him and said: "Lord, help me" (Matthew 15:25).

You would think that by now Jesus would have just healed her daughter, but He denied her request again, saying:

"It is not right to take the children's bread and toss it to their dogs."

Matthew 15:26

This was probably the most embarrassing experience the lady ever had. No amount of exegesis can erase the sting of Jesus' statement. Surely, she should now accept that her daughter would not be healed. However, she replied to the Lord in humility saying:

"Yes, Lord.....but even the dogs eat the crumbs that fall from their masters' table."

Matthew 15:27

This response is loaded! First of all, she acknowledges that Jesus is Lord. Secondly, she humbles herself by demonstrating that she is willing to accept even the crumbs that fall on the ground. Thirdly, she sees Jesus as her master, the only One to whom she could turn for any real help.

This Canaanite woman finally got the answer she desired. Take a look at what Jesus said:

"Woman, you have great faith! Your request is granted."

Matthew 15:28

Her daughter was healed! Would you be willing to go through all of what this woman went through in order to receive your healing. Hopefully your answer is a resounding 'yes'.

It is imperative that we understand that if the Lord's response seems unfavorable at first, it might not necessarily be so. Perhaps the Lord wants to stretch your faith as well as your perseverance, and deepen your resolve to seek Him with all your heart.

Keep asking the people of God to pray with you for your healing, or for the healing of your loved ones, and receive His healing touch in your life in Jesus' name.

Remember:
It is imperative that we understand that if the Lord's response seems unfavorable at first, it might not necessarily be so.

Challenge:
Memorize Matthew 7:7-8

> "Ask and it will be given to you; seek and you will find; knock and the door will be opened to you. For everyone who asks receives; he who seeks finds; and to him who knocks, the door will be opened."
>
> Matthew 7:7-8

Prayer For Today

Heavenly Father, I thank You for Your great grace to me. In my time of need, You have commanded me to call upon Your name, and I thank You for that. Thank You for calling me to prayer. You are never tired of me, neither do You reject me. I thank You for Your faithful kindness to me and Your everlasting compassion for me. I ask You, Lord, for complete healing. All these things I pray in the mighty name of Jesus.

Amen.

Divine Judgment
and Sickness

Healing From Insanity

"At the same time that my sanity was restored, my
honor and splendor were returned to me for the glory
of my kingdom. My advisers and nobles sought me
out, and I was restored to my throne and became even
greater than before. Now I, Nebuchadnezzar, praise
and exalt and glorify the King of heaven, because
everything he does is right and all his ways are just.
And those who walk in pride he is able to humble."

DANIEL 5:36-37

"You will keep in perfect peace him whose mind is
steadfast, because he trusts in you. Trust in the Lord
forever, for the Lord, the Lord is the Rock eternal."

ISAIAH 26:3-4

OUR MENTAL WELL-BEING MUST NEVER be taken for granted. In recent years,
various local churches have seen an increasing number of individuals
entering their doors with such serious mental illnesses as depression,
anxiety disorders, mild schizophrenia, eating disorders, addictive

behaviors, bipolar disorder and the like. The Church cannot afford to hold the view that such illnesses must be coped with. As it relates to the healing power of God, we cannot afford to doubt the ability of the Lord to heal and restore health to our minds.

In the Bible, the Lord restored mental health to a few individuals, and in today's devotion, we are going to look at one of those cases. This case started out with a man in his right mind who became insane and was later restored to full mental health by the Lord. His name was Nebuchadnezzar.

Nebuchadnezzar, king of Babylon, was without question the greatest leader of the Neo-Babylonian Empire. On one occasion, he had a dream that deeply disturbed him, and so he called together his wise men, magicians, enchanters, astrologers, and diviners, and told them his dream. He had hoped that they would have been able to explain its meaning, but they could not. There was, however, a wise Jew named Daniel, who had been entrusted by the Lord with the gift of interpreting dreams, and to him the king explained his dream.

Let us take a look at a few verses in the book of Daniel in order to get an idea of the dream king Nebuchadnezzar had.

"In the visions I saw while lying in my bed, I looked, and there before me was a messenger, a holy one, coming down from heaven. He called in a loud voice: 'Cut down the tree and trim off its branches; strip off its leaves and scatter its fruit. Let the animals flee from under it and the birds from its branches. But let the stump and its roots, bound with iron and bronze, remain in the ground, in the grass of the field. Let him be drenched with the dew of heaven, and let him live with the animals among the plants of the earth. Let his mind be changed from that of a man and let him be given the mind of an animal, till seven times pass by for him.'"

Daniel 4:13-16

Daniel listened carefully to what the king had told him, and the Lord gave him the meaning of the dream. The tree in Nebuchadnezzar's dream represented Nebuchadnezzar himself (Daniel 4:22). Daniel explained that the king had become so powerful that his greatness was sky high, and his authority extended to the distant parts of the earth (Daniel 4:22). He made it clear to the king that God, the Most High, had however, decreed that Nebuchadnezzar should be driven away from men and live as a wild beast for a period of seven times, (believed by scholars to be a period of seven years) (Daniel 4:25).

Daniel understood from the dream that God was divinely judging Nebuchadnezzar because of his sins, and so he pleaded with the king of Babylon, and encouraged him to renounce his sins, and do what was right (Daniel 4:27). Nebuchadnezzar, however, did not take heed to Daniel's warning, and instead, exalted himself saying:

> "Is this not the great Babylon I have built as the royal residence,
> by my mighty power and for the glory of my majesty?"
>
> Daniel 4:30

Immediately after those proud words had left the lips of king Nebuchadnezzar, he became insane (Daniel 4:31-32). His self-exaltation was the sin that literally brought a mental illness into his own life. This shows us that we should never underestimate the direct link between a sin and an illness.

When we look at Deuteronomy 28, in declaring the blessings and curses of God, Moses explained to the children of Israel that if they obeyed the Word of God, many blessings would rest upon their lives. Alternately, curses were attached to disobedience. Look at Deuteronomy 28:28:

> "The Lord will afflict you with madness, blindness and confu-
> sion of mind."

What a warning! Moses explained that curses would come upon them if they forsook the Lord. Take a look at what the Word of God says:

"The Lord will send on you curses, confusion and rebuke in everything you put your hand to, until you are destroyed and come to sudden ruin because of the evil you have done in forsaking him."

Deuteronomy 28:20

Unfortunately, though true, we live in a world where many unwittingly believe that there are no direct consequences for sinning against the Lord. The Bible unequivocally declares that this sentiment is false. Although we should not categorically state that all sickness is the due to personal sin, it must never be thought that sin and sickness are unrelated.

Nebuchadnezzar is a good reminder of what can happen to us if we exalt ourselves. We ought to be careful of making pompous self-exalting statements, for the Bible teaches us that pride goes before destruction, and a haughty spirit before a fall (Proverbs 16:18).

Thankfully, Nebuchadnezzar did not die in a state of insanity. The Bible tells us that after the period of time had elapsed, he raised his eyes toward heaven, and his sanity was restored (Daniel 4:34). So much good can occur when we humble ourselves and look to the Lord. The psalmist David declared:

"I lift up my eyes to the hills – where does my help come from? My help comes from the Lord, the Maker of heaven and earth."

Psalm 121:1-2

When we humbly look to the One who created us, we receive so much help and mercy. Let us learn from king Nebuchadnezzar and receive the divine blessing of God in our minds as we humble ourselves and look to the Lord.

Remember:
When we humbly look to the One who created us, we receive so much help and mercy.

Challenge:
Memorize Isaiah 26:3-4

> "You will keep in perfect peace him whose mind is steadfast, because he trusts in you. Trust in the Lord forever, for the Lord, the Lord is the Rock eternal."
>
> Isaiah 26:3-4

Prayer For Today

Heavenly Father, I thank You for creating me. You know every little part of me, and there is nothing about me that You do not know. You know how my mind functions, and You are able to give me a healthy mind. Dear Lord, I ask You to restore my sanity. Heal my mind, O Lord. Restore joy to me and make me rejoice, truly rejoice in You, O Lord. Stretch forth Your hand, Lord, and heal my mind in the name of Jesus, I pray.

Amen.

Don't Fight Against God

"But Elymas the sorcerer (for that is what his name means)
opposed them and tried to turn the proconsul from the
faith. Then Saul, who was called Paul, filled with the Holy
Spirit, looked straight at Elymas and said, "You are a child
of the devil and an enemy of everything that is right! You
are full of all kinds of deceit and trickery. Will you never
stop perverting the right ways of the Lord? Now the hand
of the Lord is against you. You are going to be blind, and
for a time you will be unable to see the light of the sun.""

ACTS 13:8-11A

"For, "Whoever would love life and see good days must keep his
tongue from evil and his lips from deceitful speech. He must
turn from evil and do good; he must seek peace and pursue it.""

1PETER 3:10-11

THE LORD TAKES HIS SALVIFIC work very seriously and those who try to
interfere with it bring serious harm to themselves. This thought may
sound rather surprising to some, but let us look at the true account of a
fellow called Elymas in order to get a better understanding.

Both Barnabas and Saul (also called Paul) were busy doing the work of the Lord, proclaiming the Word of God in Jewish synagogues in the town of Salamis (Acts 13:5). As they continued travelling and preaching the Word of God, they met a false prophet and Jewish sorcerer named Bar-Jesus (Acts 13:6) who was an attendant of the proconsul, Sergius Paulus. (The interpretation of the name Bar-Jesus is Elymas which means 'sorcerer' (Acts 13:8)).

Sergius sent for both Paul and Barnabas because he wished to hear the Word of God, but Elymas had other plans. He opposed both Paul and Barnabas, and tried to turn Sergius away from the faith (Acts 13:8). The apostle Paul, under the power of the Holy Spirit, looked at Elymas and exposed him for who he really was. Look at what the apostle Paul said:

> "You are a child of the devil and an enemy of everything that is right! You are full of all kinds of deceit and trickery. Will you never stop perverting the right ways of the Lord? Now the hand of the Lord is against you. You are going to be blind, and for a time you will be unable to see the light of the sun."
>
> Acts 13:10-11a

Wow! At least four awful vices were mentioned concerning Elymas, and we have to look at each one separately in order to grasp why he was divinely judged by God with an illness. Let us get straight into it!

The First Vice – He Was a Child of the Devil

The very first vice proclaimed by the apostle Paul, under the leadership of the Holy Spirit, was that Elymas was a child of the devil. This is serious! This meant that he was operating under the rule of the devil, and was working against the move of God. The devil does not advance the mission of God – the saving of lives. Instead, he opposes it. Elymas was willing to join the devil in opposing the work of God – that of enabling Sergius to come into the saving knowledge of Jesus Christ. He wanted

Sergius to remain blind to the truth of the gospel of Jesus Christ, and he himself was physically blinded by the divine judgment of God.

The Second Vice – He Was an Enemy of Everything That Was Right

Secondly, the apostle Paul declared that Elymas was an enemy of everything that was right (Acts 13:10). This is awful! Being an enemy of everything that was right meant that Elymas was in total agreement with everything that was evil. He was hostile to the truth of the Word of God, and his hostility was shown in his attempt to turn Sergius away from the knowledge of the Lord.

It makes no sense to fight against the Lord – you can never win that battle. Instead, what occurs is that you forfeit God's great mercy and healing in your life.

The Third Vice – He Was Full of Deceit and Trickery

The third feature of Elymas that we must consider is that he was full of all kinds of deceit and trickery (Acts 13:10). Deceitfulness can prevent us from receiving anything good from the Lord. Look at what the Word of God declares:

> "For, "Whoever would love life and see good days must keep his tongue from evil and his lips from deceitful speech. He must turn from evil and do good; he must seek peace and pursue it.""
>
> 1Peter 3:10-11

The Word of God makes it abundantly clear that seeing good days is linked to godly speech. Elymas' speech was filled with ungodliness. His entire life was filled with lies, and the result was blindness.

The Fourth Vice – He Perverted the Right Ways of the Lord

Elymas' fourth vice was perverting the right ways of the Lord (Acts 13:10). This meant that he would twist the truth of God's Word. Twisting biblical truth is frequently done by individuals who have a hidden agenda.

There are people who do not believe in the healing power of God, and so they twist the scriptures to fit their erroneous point of view. They attempt to distort the Word of God by belittling the miraculous power of God, and they try to teach Christians to cope with their illnesses, and not expect the Lord to heal them. Elymas was one who would distort the Scriptures, and it only brought harm to himself.

When we hear the Word of God, we must be vigilant not to misrepresent it or ridicule it. Take a look at what Proverbs 9:12 declares:

"If you are a mocker, you alone will suffer."

Proverbs 9:12

Elymas was the only one who suffered at the end of the day. He tried to blind the proconsul to the truth and he instead became blinded by the hand of God. Ironically, the proconsul actually surrendered his life to the Lord. Elymas tried to oppose the work of God and instead, he was opposed by God. He tried to pervert the truth of God's Word, but the Word of God still went forth and birthed fruit.

Let us see to it that we are not standing in opposition to the work of the Lord while simultaneously praying for the Lord to heal us.

Remember:
When we hear the Word of God, we must be vigilant not to misrepresent it or ridicule it.

Challenge:
Memorize 1 Peter 3:10-11

"For, "Whoever would love life and see good days must keep his tongue from evil and his lips from deceitful speech. He must turn from evil and do good; he must seek peace and pursue it.""

1Peter 3:10-11

PRAYER FOR TODAY

Heavenly Father, I thank You for Your Word. Help me not to oppose Your truth in any way whatsoever. Help me to accept and believe Your Word whenever You speak. I do not want to oppose Your truth in my life, or to encourage others to oppose Your truth. I thank You for Your powerful Word in my life. Help me to accept and to hold on to Your Word always. Forgive me, Lord, for the times I have not willingly accepted Your truth. Even now, I ask You to fill me with an insatiable desire for Your Word, and to make me delight in it with all my heart, soul, mind and strength. All these things I pray in the mighty name of Jesus.

Amen.

DAY 15

Sexual Sin and Suffering

"I have given her time to repent of her immorality, but
she is unwilling. So I will cast her on a bed of suffering,
and I will make those who commit adultery with her
suffer intensely, unless they repent of her ways."

REVELATION 2:21-22

"What shall we say, then? Shall we go on sinning
so that grace may increase? By no means! We died
to sin; how can we live in it any longer?

ROMANS 6:1-2

ONE OF THE MOST TERRIFYING rebukes given by the Lord is found in the book of Revelation. In the first three chapters of that book, Jesus addressed the seven churches of Asia Minor, one of which was the church in Thyatira (Revelation 2:18-29). His address began in a fairly complementary manner, but it quickly escalated into a scathing rebuke to which we would do well to give some attention.

The problem with the church at Thyatira emerged as a result of a compromising leader and a self- professed prophetess. For some odd reason, the leader of the church in Thyatira had allowed this woman to have a teaching position in the church, and Jesus, the Savior of the church, did not approve of this decision at all. In the eyes of the Lord, she was not a prophetess, but an unbelieving Jezebel. That is not my opinion, the Lord actually called her Jezebel.

In the book of Kings we are told of Jezebel and her most notorious act – that of introducing Baal-worship into Israel as a national religion. She had filled the land of Israel with her false gods and false prophets, having made it her goal to lead Israel away from Yahweh, the only true God.

The spirit of Jezebel was active in the church of Thyatira through this self-proclaimed prophetess. In the same way that Jezebel had led Ahab, her husband, into idolatry, this woman had exalted herself to the position of prophetess and somehow managed to influence the pastoral leader of the church to give her a teaching position there. Although she had the responsibility of teaching the people of God, there was something fundamentally wrong with her teaching which led the people of God into sexual sin, and in eating food sacrificed to idols. How could that be? Let me be very clear – she was not teaching the Word of God. 2 Timothy 3:16 declares:

> "All Scripture is God-breathed and is useful for teaching, rebuking, correcting and training in righteousness."

When the local church ceases to preach the Word of God, we are open to pleasant-sounding words that have no power or authority to rebuke us into repentance. This self-professed prophetess, this 'Jezebel', was teaching in church, but she was not teaching God's mighty Word. She taught her own views, and, as a result, God's people were led into sexual immorality and idolatry.

The Lord gave her a chance to repent of her immorality, but the Bible tells us that she was unwilling to repent (Revelation 2:21). Imagine that! God's abundant mercy was extended to her, but she refused to turn from her sinful ways.

When we refuse to repent of our sins, we will be disciplined by God, and often this involves terrible sickness. Take a look at what Jesus said as a result of her unrepentance:

> "So I will cast her on a bed of suffering, and I will make those who commit adultery with her suffer intensely, unless they repent of her ways."
>
> Revelation 2:22

We should never ignore the fact that certain illnesses are directly related to unrepentant sin. No amount of prayer and Bible reading will do us any good as long as we are knowingly engaging in unrepentant sin. This woman could have been healed IF only she had turned from her sins!

I would like to reiterate the point that we cannot experience God's mighty healing power while deliberately living in disobedience. There are those who believe that God's grace covers our presumptuous and unrepentant sin, but do not be fooled. The Bible says:

> "For the grace of God that brings salvation has appeared to all men. It teaches us to say "No" to ungodliness and worldly passions, and to live self-controlled, upright and godly lives in this present age."
>
> Titus 2:11-12

God's grace gives us the power to say "No" to sin, **not to live in sin**. If we turn away from our sins and put Jesus first, beautiful things will happen in our lives.

The Lord has given us time to repent, and we must take advantage of this opportunity we have received. If you are currently sick and you believe that it could be linked to your own disobedience, please take the time to speak to the Lord. One thing we all should never forget – God is merciful. The Bible declares:

"For the Lord is good; his mercy is everlasting."

Psalm 100:5

The Lord gave an ultimatum to the church of Thyatira:

"... I will make those who commit adultery with her suffer intensely, unless they repent of her ways."

Revelation 2:22b

Repentance prevents us from receiving the divine judgment of God. Let us willingly turn from every offensive way, and walk in obedience to the Word of the Lord.

Remember:
The Lord has given us time to repent, and we must take advantage of this opportunity we have received.

Challenge:
Memorize Romans 6:1-2

"What shall we say, then? Shall we go on sinning so that grace may increase? By no means! We died to sin; how can we live in it any longer?

Romans 6:1-2

PRAYER FOR TODAY

Heavenly Father, I thank You for Your abounding mercies towards me. Help me to take full advantage of Your mercy, Lord. I repent of every sinful direction in which I have walked. Forgive me, Lord, for walking in a manner contrary to Your truth. You have called me to be holy, and I renounce every offensive way, and I recommit my walk to You. Again,

Lord I ask You to wash me in Your precious blood and cleanse me from all unrighteousness. May my life be one that always brings glory to Your name and never shame.

All these things I pray in the name of Jesus.

Amen.

An Unholy Communion

"A man ought to examine himself before he eats of the
bread and drinks of the cup. For anyone who eats and drinks
without recognizing the body of the Lord eats and drinks
judgment on himself. That is why many among you are
weak and sick, and a number of you have fallen asleep."

1 Corinthians 11:28-30

"Therefore confess your sins to each other and pray
for each other so that you may be healed. The prayer
of a righteous man is powerful and effective."

James 5:16

In our quest to understand more about what our Lord and Savior has
said about healing, we need to consider possible reasons, based on the
Word of God, why someone may be sick. The Scriptures give us examples of believers who were sick as a direct result of God's divine judgment, and we would do well to learn from their lives. Never ignore or
take lightly the warnings given to us in the Word of God explaining why
someone was ill.

Today, we are going to look at a warning which was given to the Church in Corinth. Though it was a community of believers in Jesus Christ, there were many problems – including discord, self-interest, inconsiderate behavior, self-indulgence, pride and sexual immorality, just to name a few. It is no wonder that many scholars have always referred to this church as the 'carnal' church.

By now we should all know that the Lord never allows His church to grow in a sinful direction - He disciplines his beloved church, (Hebrews 12:6) and He tells us why. Take a look at what the word of God says:

"... God disciplines us for our good, that we may share in his holiness."

Hebrews 12:10

The ultimate goal of the discipline of the Lord, is for us to share in His holiness. However, this only occurs as we become more like our Savior Jesus Christ. Therefore, God disciplines us in order for us to grow into Christlikeness so that we may be holy as He is holy. May we never forget that!

Unfortunately, the church of Corinth was not growing in the holiness of the Lord. Instead, they were steeped in sinful practices (1 Corinthians 11:18-22). What made it worse, was that they were also taking the Lord's Supper, and as a result, some of the believers were judged by the Lord with sickness and death.

The Lord's supper, (popularly known as Communion in some churches today), was a service for remembering what Jesus had done for His people, when He laid down His life on the cross. The Bible says:

"For whenever you eat this bread and drink this cup, you proclaim the Lord's death until he comes."

1 Corinthians 11:26

The death of Christ was sacrificial, but the attitude of some of the members of the Corinthian church was selfish. The Lord's death was one of selflessness, and this was in contrast to the self-indulgent attitude of the various members of the Corinthian church. Although the Lord's death showed the mercy of God, the attitude of many members was filled with impatience and indifference. Finally, the death of Christ showed the love of God, but the love of some of the members of the Corinthian church fell far short of what the Lord had expected of them.

Somehow the act of sharing in the Lord's Supper had lost its meaning, and the members were simply going through the motions without any heart for the Lord. This hypocrisy had led them to eat and drink judgment on themselves. Those are not my words! Look at what the Bible says:

"For anyone who eats and drinks without recognizing the body of the Lord eats and drinks judgment on himself."

1 Corinthians 11:29

As a result of God's judgment on the church of Corinth, many members became physically weak and sick, and several actually died. Look again at what the Bible says:

"That is why many among you are weak and sick, and a number of you have fallen asleep."

1 Corinthians 11:30

Sometimes sickness occurs in the lives of believers because of God's divine discipline, and unfortunately, the Corinthian Church learned this lesson the hard way. Let us all learn from this church, so that we do not have the same fate.

The chapters in this section have not been written to scare you. Instead, I want you to be aware of the very real relationship between sin and sickness. The healing power of God is always available to those who walk in His holy Word. When the Holy Spirit convicts us of sin, let us quickly repent of it and turn to the Lord, and allow the powerful blood of Jesus to cleanse us and bring healing to our lives.

Remember:

By now we should all know that the Lord never allows His church to grow in a sinful direction - He disciplines his beloved church.

Challenge:

1.   Have you been living in a compromising situation while partaking in the Lord's Supper? If you have, please be open and confess your sins to a godly leader.
2.   **Memorize James 5:16**

"Therefore confess your sins to each other and pray for each other so that you may be healed. The prayer of a righteous man is powerful and effective."

James 5:16

Prayer For Today

Heavenly Father, I thank You for Your faithfulness in my life. You have never left me to myself when I am moving in the wrong direction. Instead, You have repeatedly convicted me and called me back to the truth of Your holy Word. Thank You, Lord, for Your mercy. Forgive me of all my sins and give me a repentant heart. May all sin become increasingly sinful to me as I seek Your face. Even now, Lord, I commit my walk to You, and I renounce all that is offensive to You. Strengthen me, Lord, and help me to honor Your name. Thank You for Your forgiveness. Thank You for reaching out to me and letting me experience Your call on my life. I thank You for saving me, Lord, and for giving me an abundant life. All these things I pray in the name of Jesus.

Amen.

Not All Sickness Is Linked To Sin

It Was For God's Glory

"As he went along, he saw a man blind from birth. His
disciples asked him, "Rabbi, who sinned, this man or his
parents, that he was born blind?" "Neither this man nor
his parents sinned," said Jesus, "but this happened so
that the work of God might be displayed in his life."

JOHN 9:1-3

THERE ARE SEVERAL INDIVIDUALS WHO believe that every sickness is somehow
connected to a sin committed by the sick person or by a close relative.
Although we do have biblical examples of generational curses in the
form of sicknesses (for example Gehazi, and his family line), it would
be totally wrong to assume that every illness is linked to a sin or generational curse.

Jesus' disciples had such a mistaken belief as it related to illnesses.
On one occasion, they saw a man who was born blind, and they asked
Jesus a rather interesting question:

"........ Rabbi, who sinned, this man or his parents, that he was
born blind?"

John 9:2

In their eyes, the blindness was either linked to some wrong he had committed or, more accurately, to a sin his parents had committed before he was conceived. In the disciples' minds, there must have been a reason God allowed this man to be blind, and as far as they were concerned, it could only have been grounded in sin. But they were wrong! While no one can deny the direct association between sin and sickness, it is important to remember that not all illnesses are linked to a sin committed. Jesus had to inform his disciples that sometimes God allows a condition in our lives in order to demonstrate a quality about Himself.

Unknown to the disciples, and all who knew him, this blind man had a purpose in God's plan. Imagine that! This seemingly terrible situation in which this man was born was meant by God to show the world that nothing is beyond the power of God. He was literally born that way so that the Lord could display His healing power through him. Take a look at what Jesus said to his disciples:

> "Neither this man nor his parents sinned," said Jesus, "but this happened so that the work of God might be displayed in his life."
>
> John 9:3

I love Jesus' words! There are many who do not believe in the power of God, and so He mercifully works through our sicknesses and disabilities to show a lost and unbelieving world that He is mighty and able to heal every single illness.

Jesus was not about to leave this man in his blind state. He spat on the ground, made mud with His saliva, and placed it on the man's eyes (John 9:6). We were formed by the Lord from the dust of the earth, and here, Jesus showed Himself to be the Creator by taking lifeless dirt, mixing it with His saliva and remaking this man's eyes. Amazing! Only the good Lord Jesus can take lifeless materials and bring life to the dead parts of our bodies!

One final thought! Before this blind man was totally healed, Jesus told him to go and wash in the pool of Siloam. He obeyed, and His eyes were opened (John 9:7). We must never overlook the 'small' instructions given to us by the Lord. When we call out to the Lord for healing, and He gives us a little instruction, we must always obey.

The Lord is still in the business of opening blind eyes, dissolving cataracts, and demonstrating that He alone is the Great Healer. Put your complete trust in Him and may He touch your eyes and cause you to experience the life-breathing power of His healing touch.

Remember:

There are many who do not believe in the power of God, and so He mercifully works through our sicknesses and disabilities to show a lost and unbelieving world that He is mighty and able to heal every single illness.

Challenge:
Memorize John 9:3

"Neither this man nor his parents sinned," said Jesus, "but this happened so that the work of God might be displayed in his life."

John 9:3

Prayer For Today

Heavenly Father, You are so great. I thank You for having a purpose for my life. Help me to remember that You are using every condition in my life to bring glory to Your name. Indeed, Lord, my life is for Your glory, and may my life continually be used to bring glory to Your name. Please use my life Lord, to help others see how great You are. In the midst of my situation, Lord, I will continually lift up Your holy name. Thank You, Lord, for healing me, strengthening me and for bringing me out of my situation. Oh, Lord, I praise You. All these things I pray in the name of Jesus.

Amen.

The Power Of Jesus' Name

Through Faith In Jesus' Name

> "By faith in the name of Jesus, this man whom you
> see and know was made strong. It is Jesus' name and
> the faith that comes through him that has given this
> complete healing to him, as you can all see."

ACTS 3:16

> "He called his twelve disciples to him and gave them authority
> to drive out evil spirits and to heal every disease and sickness."

MATTHEW 10:1

THERE IS TREMENDOUS AUTHORITY IN the name of Jesus! Satan and his army of demons tremble at the sound of His name; diseases are expelled from bodies; ailments are healed, and salvation is given to all who believe in the matchless name of Jesus. Our Savior is immeasurably powerful, and nothing is impossible for Him.

The apostles were men who were completely convinced of the power of the name of Jesus. Under the influence of the Holy Spirit, they spoke the Word of God with great conviction, fully aware that everything had to submit to the authority of the Name, Jesus. This is wonderfully conveyed in the account given to us in Acts 3.

On one occasion, the apostles Peter and John were on their way to their daily prayer meeting and a man who had been crippled from birth begged them for some money. Unknown to him, Peter and John were not ordinary temple-going folk, but prayerful men who were filled with the Holy Spirit and a deep devotion to Jesus. They both had a life-breathing relationship with the Lord and had much more to give than a few bucks. It is necessary for me to comment here and state that we often act in the same way as this blind man did. Not being cognizant of how low our expectations are, we end up asking for inconsequential things that are of little or no benefit to us. Further, our lack of spiritual discernment blinds us from realizing how close we are to a life-changing encounter. This crippled man had grown so accustomed to his forty-year condition, that his entire worldview had been colored by his painful life- experiences. He saw himself as just an unfortunate beggar who was dependent on whatever was given to him. As Christians, we can find ourselves suffering from this defeatist mindset when we allow our minds to be shaped by our experiences, rather than by the Word of God. Regardless of how awful our life experiences have been, God's Word has the power to renew our minds, transform our lives, and break the stronghold of false belief systems.

There is another aspect we must consider as it relates to this crippled man. He was encouraged to remain in his crippled condition by those who entered the temple. Day after day, temple-going folk passed him by, comfortably entering the temple. As far as they were concerned, they could only be sympathetic to him and give him a few dollars whenever they could. As believers in Christ, we cannot afford to be like the many who easily pass by those in desperate need of the healing power of God, and miss the opportunity to be used by God to impact the lives of others. The Lord wants to demonstrate His mighty healing power in the lives of those who are sick, and He waits patiently for an opportunity to show forth His power in their lives. The Lord allowed both Peter and John to cross the path of this crippled man. When he saw them, he begged them for money, but little did he know that he was in for a big surprise. With authority, Peter responded to his petition, saying:

> "Silver and gold I do not have, but what I have I give you. In the name of Jesus Christ of Nazareth, walk."
>
> Acts 3:6

Jesus changed his life, and he walked for the first time in forty years. He was so filled with joy that he went into the temple courts walking, jumping and praising God (Acts 3:8). It was a wonderful miracle! This crippled man, who had no other purpose than to beg, was healed and became a powerful instrument in the hand of the Lord. All those people who were mere temple-goers became true believers under the mighty preaching of Peter, and this once helpless man was instrumental in their spiritual transformation.

Over and over, we see throughout God's Word that God's healing is not only for ourselves, but it plays a mighty role in encouraging unbelievers to come into the saving knowledge of the true and living God. This is why I will always encourage you to make your healing public. Always resolve in your heart to publicly declare that Jesus has healed you!

Remember:
As Christians, we can find ourselves suffering from this defeatist mindset when we allow our minds to be shaped by our experiences, rather than by the Word of God.

Challenge:
Memorize Acts 3:16

> "By faith in the name of Jesus, this man whom you see and know was made strong. It is Jesus' name and the faith that comes

through him that has given this complete healing to him, as you can all see."

Acts 3:16

PRAYER FOR TODAY

Heavenly Father, I thank You for being the Great Healer. You have healed in the days of old, and You are still doing the same thing today. I put my faith in Your great name, and I ask You, Lord, to heal me of every sickness, infirmity, and disease in the powerful name of Jesus. Make me strong, Lord, and grant me complete healing. All these things I ask You in the mighty name of Jesus.

Amen.

Just Ask Jesus

Bring The 'Small' Things Also

"Jesus left the synagogue and went to the home of
Simon. Now Simon's mother-in-law was suffering from
a high fever, and they asked Jesus to help her. So he
bent over her and rebuked the fever, and it left her.
She got up at once and began to wait on them."

LUKE 4:38-39

"His father was sick in bed, suffering from fever and dysentery.
Paul went in to see him and, after prayer, placed his hands
on him and healed him. When this had happened, the
rest of the sick on the island came and were cured."

ACTS 28:8-9

IT WOULD NOT BE FARFETCHED to assume that we have all had an unwel-
comed encounter with a fever. We know how awful it can be. Our body
temperature increases, we experience fatigue, joint pains, nausea, and,
if the fever lasts for a long time, we can feel unbearably cold – just thinking about it reminds me of how dreadful it can be. No one in their right
mind enjoys having a fever!

Perhaps the most reassuring aspect of having a fever is knowing it is going to pass, and oftentimes, quite quickly. Some would never think of praying for the Lord's healing of a fever, as it could seem too small a request, and the thought might simply be to let it run its course. After all, it is just a fever – quite a small sickness to bring to God in prayer. Wrong!

Frequently, we can be misled into thinking that the Lord solely cares about the 'major' sicknesses such as cancer, AIDS, severe diabetes, and the like. It is important, however, for us to be repeatedly reminded that the good Lord cares deeply for us, and is concerned about our health, even when we have a comparatively minor illness, like a fever. Never forget, the Lord's desire for all His children is that they are in good health (3 John 2).

Jesus definitely has no trouble healing the 'little' sicknesses in our lives, such as fevers. I especially love that the Lord is not only able, but willing to heal every sickness and disease when we bring it to His attention. On one occasion, Simon's mother-in-law suffered from a high fever and Jesus was asked to help her (Luke 4:38), and He did!

In today's devotion, we are going to look at three lessons we can take away from this little account.

Our First Lesson – Bring Every Matter to the Lord In Prayer
We have often heard that there is no situation that is *too big* for the Lord, but we also need to hear that there is no situation that is *too small* for the Lord. In the big problems, we have no choice but to look to the Lord, but in the little things, we face the temptation of not taking the problem to Him at all. We reason to ourselves that we can simply go to the pharmacy and pick up a pain-killer and we will be fine. While I am not suggesting that we should avoid using the medicinal options available to us, we must also remember that we have direct access to the Lord. Even when we use medication for our healing, praying to the Lord should still be our first priority.

The Word of God encourages us to bring everything to the Lord in prayer:

"Do not be anxious about anything, but in everything, by prayer and petition, with thanksgiving, present your requests to God"

Philippians 4:6

I have found that many believers struggle to pray and ask the Lord for good things. As a matter of fact, some have openly confessed their lack of expectation of good things from the Lord. This is nothing but a satanic attack on the minds and lives of professing Christians. We should expect nothing else but good from the Lord. When the Lord created the world, each day he declared: 'It was good'. The Psalmist David knew of the goodness of the Lord when he penned these words – 'goodness and mercy shall follow me all the days of my life' (Psalm 23:6). Again, the Word clearly declares: "For the Lord is good" (Psalm 100:3a). It will be difficult, if not impossible to ask the Lord to do anything good in our lives if we fail to believe the truth about who He is – He is GOOD! The people who asked Jesus to look at Simon's mother- in-law knew about the goodness of Jesus, and so they had no trouble asking Him to do a good thing – to heal this woman.

Our Second Lesson – Jesus Healed After They Made Their Request
There are some people who believe that if the Lord wants them healed they will be healed no matter what. That is certainly not true! Please note that Jesus did not heal this woman without first being asked. Take a look at what the Bible declares:

"You do not have because you do not ask"

James 4:2

The Lord has made it clear that we do not have, because we fail to ask. Prayer, which was beautifully defined by Dr. Stanley D. Toussaint as asking God for something, opens the door for receiving what God can do in our lives. The Lord responds when we pray. We are praying to a living, able, powerful and Almighty God who answers us WHEN WE PRAY!

When you call upon the name of the Lord, expect Him to answer. When you ask Him to heal your body, expect Him to move mightily. Jesus responded to their requests and He still responds today – when we pray!

Our Third Lesson – Jesus Holds All Authority
Jesus, the only One who can save, holds ALL authority. Did you notice that Jesus did not ask the fever to leave the woman's body? He rebuked it! He told the fever to correct itself, and guess what? It obeyed Jesus, and left her body. A sickness cannot do what it wants irrespective of what Jesus has said. Jesus has authority over every sickness, and so every sickness must obey His command.

Please pray and ask the good Lord to heal you. Ask Him to touch your body with His mighty power and heal every part of your being.

Remember:
The people who asked Jesus to look at Simon's mother-in-law knew about the goodness of Jesus, and so they had no trouble asking Him to do a good thing – to heal this woman.

Challenge:
Memorize Luke 4:38-39

> Jesus left the synagogue and went to the home of Simon. Now Simon's mother-in-law was suffering from a high fever, and they asked Jesus to help her. So he bent over her and rebuked the fever, and it left her. She got up at once and began to wait on them."
>
> Luke 4:38-39

PRAYER FOR TODAY
Heavenly Father, I thank You for being such a good and wonderful Father. I confess, Lord, that there are times that I struggle to believe

that You will do good to me. Forgive me, Lord, for denying Your immeasurable goodness in my life. Forgive me, Lord, for failing to ask You to heal my body. Even now, Father, in the name of Jesus, I ask You to stretch forth Your mighty hand and heal me. You hold all power and authority, Lord, and I come to You, the Almighty God, for only You can heal me. I thank You for Your healing touch in my life, Lord. All these things I pray in Jesus' name.

Amen.

The Lord Heals Barren Wombs

> "Early the next morning they arose and worshipped before the
> Lord and then went back to their home at Ramah. Elkanah lay
> with Hannah his wife, and the Lord remembered her. So in the
> course of time Hannah conceived and gave birth to a son. She
> named him Samuel, saying, "Because I asked the Lord for him.""

1 SAMUEL 1:19-20

PERHAPS ONE OF THE MOST challenging situations for a young married couple to face is finding out that they cannot have children. Various emotions can play on the couple's mind, particularly if there was sexual immorality before marriage or some other sinful act such as an abortion. Our past, can definitely make us experience intense feelings of guilt, and often we feel completely unworthy to ask the Lord to bring healing to our lives. It is remarkable how easy it is for us to entertain self-defeating thoughts when we find ourselves in the grip of a disappointment, and even if we do not experience feelings of guilt, we may silently wonder why the Lord has withheld such wonderful gifts from our lives.

The Bible contains several examples of married couples who could not have children, one of them being Hannah and Elkanah. Their marriage was not ideal in light of the fact that Elkanah had two wives. Yes, you read that correctly. Elkanah was married to both Hannah and Peninnah, and as you might imagine, there was a lot of tension in that family. The wives did not get along, as Elkanah made it clear that he loved Hannah more than Peninnah. Needless to say, this made Peninnah extremely jealous, and she would retaliate by mercilessly taunting Hannah about her inability to become pregnant, making her deeply sad.

Year after year, Peninnah would continually tease Hannah, leaving her distraught and upset. On one occasion, however, instead of just feeling sorry for herself, Hannah decided to do something different – she took her childless condition to the Lord in prayer (1 Samuel 1:10). She did not wait until there was a glimmer of hope, or until her rival had made peace with her, no, she prayed while she was in bitter distress.

As believers in Christ, we must learn to see our problems as opportunities to call upon the name of the Lord. Take a look at what the Bible says:

"Is any one of you in trouble? He should pray."

James 5:13

While Hannah was in a difficult position, she prayed to the Lord, and she promised Him that if He blessed her with a son, she would dedicate him to the service of the Lord (1 Samuel 1:11). I firmly believe that the Lord loves these kinds of prayers. Hannah was not making an egoistic prayer. She was not merely asking for a child to stop her rival from teasing her or some other self-centered reason. She prayed for a child, and promised to give him up completely for the glory of the Lord. When we are serious about giving glory to God, we can rest assured that every prayer will be answered in the affirmative.

Hannah continued to worship the Lord after she had finished praying (1 Samuel 1:19), and the Bible tells us that the Lord heard her prayer, healed her barren womb and blessed her with a son, whom she named Samuel. (Interestingly, in the course of time, Hannah actually had seven sons (1 Samuel 2:5)).

Hannah and Elkanah were not the only couple in the Bible who had trouble having children. Abraham and Sarah, Isaac and Rebekah, Jacob and Rachel, Elizabeth and Zechariah all had trouble having a child, but the good Lord came through for every one of them. God healed the barren wombs in the days of old, and He still heals today, Hallelujah!

Remember:
As believers in Christ, we must learn to see our problems as opportunities to call upon the name of the Lord.

Challenge:
Memorize James 5:13

> "Is any one of you in trouble? He should pray. Is anyone happy?
> Let him sing songs of praise."
>
> James 5:13

PRAYER FOR TODAY

Heavenly Father, I thank You for Your faithful and persistent command for me to cry out to You. I thank You for giving me the freedom to call upon Your name, and also, for giving me peace when I pray to You – peace that is beyond human comprehension. There are certain problems that I have to face, Lord, that only You can fix. And so I come to You, Lord. I look to You in absolute desperation. Even now, Lord, I ask You to heal me in every way. You have given me Your Word, showing me that You are able and willing to do in me as You have done in the days of old. I lift up my eyes to You, Lord, and I ask You to set me free from every single thing that is not in accordance with Your will. You are the Great Healer and I will always look to You, Lord. I thank You for all that You have done so far in my life, and I thank You for Your mighty touch in my life. All these things I pray in the name of Jesus.

Amen.

Ask and Keep On Asking

"O Lord my God, I called to you for help and you healed me."

PSALM 30:2

"Then Jesus told his disciples a parable to show them
that they should always pray and not give up."

LUKE 18:1

'WHAT A FRIEND WE HAVE in Jesus,' written by Joseph M. Scriven, is one of my favorite hymns. It beautifully encourages us to bring all that we are going through to the Lord in prayer. The first stanza says:

> What a friend we have in Jesus, All our sins and griefs to bear
> What a privilege to carry, everything to God in Prayer!
> O what peace we often forfeit, O what needless pain we bear,
> All because we do not carry, everything to God in prayer!

Prayer, persistent prayer, is absolutely necessary in our walk with the Lord. We serve an awesome God who is able to do the impossible. However, we will never experience His move in our lives if we fail to call upon His name. It is highly unfortunate that the prayer meeting in the typical local church today is the least favored and most neglected service. This ubiquitous disinterest in prayer among many professing Christians implies that we do not truly believe that prayer changes things. That is very disturbing.

Throughout the Word of God we are encouraged to pray about everything. Why? Because nothing is too hard for the Lord (Genesis 18:14). He is able to save, restore, heal, deliver and rescue us, irrespective of what we are going through, and He demonstrates His mighty power in the lives of those who are faithful in prayer.

On one occasion, Jesus wanted to teach His disciples that they should not give up, but persist in prayer. He therefore told them a parable about a persistent widow and a judge who had no fear of God or care for mankind. The widow needed justice, and went to the judge for help. Her pleas, however, fell on deaf ears. Instead of feeling sorry for herself, or wasting her energy complaining about the unfair situation she was in, she made up her mind to keep going back to the unjust judge. Eventually, the judge realized that she was not going to stop coming to him until she got justice, and he reasoned to himself that it was best to give her a favorable answer in order to avoid being further bothered by her.

Jesus used this parable to teach his disciples that God the Father, the just Judge, would always come through for His children who persistently cry out to Him (Luke 18:7). That is the kind of prayer life we need in order to see the floodgates of heaven open in our midst – day and night prayer!

The widow eventually received justice because of her persistence. She focused on the fact that only the judge could grant her the justice she needed and she kept presenting her case before him, pleading for a favorable outcome – and her persistence was eventually rewarded.

The Lord rewards our faithful prayer requests. Take a look at what the Bible says:

"Ask and it shall be given to you; seek and you will find; knock and the door will be opened to you. For everyone who asks receives; he who seeks finds; and to him who knocks, the door will be opened."

Matthew 7:7-8

We all have to learn to hold on to the promises of God that are clearly expressed in His Word. Our asking is not in vain, neither is our seeking or our knocking. God wants us to pray to Him. He boldly declares:

"Call to me and I will answer you and tell you great and unsearchable things you do not know"

Jeremiah 33:3

May our faithful God, bring His mighty healing power in your life today as you call upon His powerful name, asking Him to heal your body in the name of Jesus.

Remember:
Jesus used this parable to teach his disciples that God the Father, the just Judge, would always come through for His children who persistently cry out to Him (Luke 18:7).

Challenge:
Memorize Psalm 30:2

"O Lord my God, I called to you for help and you healed me."

Psalm 30:2

PRAYER FOR TODAY

Heavenly Father, I thank You for Your great love for me. Thank You for calling me to a life of prayer, and I also thank You for answering me when I call to You. To call upon Your name is certainly not a vain activity. Forgive me, Lord, for the times I have allowed discouragement to stop me from being persistent in prayer. Today, Lord, I commit to a life of prayer, and I humbly ask You to heal my body of all sickness. I thank You, Lord, for Your gracious hand upon my life and for all Your mercies towards me. Thank You for healing me, Lord Jesus. All these things I pray in the matchless name of Jesus.

Amen.

EPILOGUE

As you come to the end of this journey, I hope you have grown to believe in the healing power of the living God, and that you have also experienced His glorious healing touch upon your body, mind and soul.

If, at this point, you have not yet been healed in your body, I encourage you not to lose hope. Go over the material again, and please allow these three individuals to encourage you: The woman with the issue of blood, Aeneas and the daughter of Abraham who had been bent over for eighteen years. You will notice that all three of them had been sick for a long time, but the Lord eventually healed them. A long time can sometimes feel like the Lord is saying 'no'. However, I encourage you to stand upon the Biblical testimony of those whom the Lord has touched, and not on your feelings.

Please allow these two verses to encourage you to continue asking the Lord to heal you:

> "Great crowds came to him, bringing the lame, the blind, the crippled, the mute and many others, and laid them at his feet; and he healed them. The people were amazed when they saw the mute speaking, the crippled made well, the lame walking and the blind seeing. And they praised the God of Israel."
>
> Matthew 15:30-31

May God richly bless you, and use you to help many others experience His healing power in their lives.

21 Days To Sexual Purity: A Biblical Devotional For Overcoming Sexual Temptations.

21 Days To Forgiveness: A Biblical Devotional For Overcoming Yesterday's Hurts.

21 Days To Knowing God's Will: A Biblical Devotional For Discovering Your God-given Purpose.

21 Days To Overcoming Procrastination: A Biblical Devotional For Achieving Far More Than You Ever Thought Possible.

Printed in Great Britain
by Amazon

42801419R00069